Sense and Nonsense

Also by Claire Crowther

Stretch of Closures (2007)
The Clockwork Gift (2009)
On Narrowness (2015)
Solar Cruise (2020)
A Pair of Three (2022)
Real Lear: New and Selected Poems (2024)

Sense and Nonsense

Essays & Interviews

Claire Crowther

edited by Carrie Etter

Shearsman Books

First published in the United Kingdom in 2024 by
Shearsman Books Ltd
PO Box 4239
Swindon
SN3 9FN

Shearsman Books Ltd Registered Office
30–31 St. James Place, Mangotsfield, Bristol BS16 9JB
(this address not for correspondence)

ISBN 978-1-84861-947-0

Acknowledgements

For permission to quote from Lorine Niedecker's work in this volume,
we are grateful to Bob Arnold, Literary Executor for the Estate
of Lorine Niedecker.

Contents

II. Interviews

Foreword

Since the publication of her first collection, *Stretch of Closures* (Shearsman, 2007), Claire Crowther has established herself as an original and distinctive poet and critic. The simultaneous publication of *Real Lear: New and Selected Poems* and this volume of essays, reviews, and interviews presents a timely consolidation of Crowther's poetry and poetics. Three threads unite to illuminate her work: a modernist approach to the use of language and form; a long-standing interest in Nonsense poetry; and an increasing use of syllabics. These elements combine to create a singular, compelling body of work which reaches a new height in the 'Real Lear' sequence of her most recent poems.

An understanding of Crowther's modernist-inflected poetics emerges through her essays on Lorine Niedecker and Veronica Forrest-Thomson. 'On the Fall in Lorine Niedecker's Poetry' steadily elucidates how Niedecker's 'condensery' or distillation operates through ellipsis, allusion, the use of the line (including length, position on the page, and enjambment), and the open field of the page. The work of condensation is also the work of articulating the lived conjunction of mental and physical experience, less explanatory than experiential. To point to just one of many examples of how this tenet informs Crowther's work, the poem 'Lost Child' from *Stretch of Closures* presents the search for the titular missing child, but ends not with a conclusion to the story, whether the child was ultimately discovered, but an evocative suggestion of the speaker's experience of the event: 'My ear is like a shell the wind swept' (28). Hence Crowther's poetry possesses a strong cinematic quality, not just in its choice of imagery but also in how the poem uses form and technique to convey aspects of experience much like the use of a cine-camera: slow or accelerating motion, zooming in or zooming out, jump-cuts (of which the above might be regarded an example), and so on.

A fuller account of Crowther's poetics materialises in her essay, 'Veronica Forrest-Thomson, Modernism, and Me'. Therein Crowther discusses finding theoretical and practical underpinnings for her emerging poetics in Forrest-Thomson's *Collected Poems* and *Poetic Artifice: A Theory of Twentieth-Century Poetry*. Forrest-Thomson's work supports Crowther's own inclination toward a poetics of linguistic and syntactic complexity (as opposed to a poetry that can be reduced to storyline or paraphrase), which appears explicated by both Forrest-Thomson's theoretical writing and poetic practice. This concurrence proves crucial for Crowther's process, from an appreciation of Forrest-Thomson's articulation of 'image-complexes' and 'bad naturalisation' to its manifestation in her poem 'Zettel'.[1] While she does in a sense 'write poems about life', Crowther nonetheless does so not through chronological narrative, but a more nuanced, less explicit evocation.

The second important thread for appreciating Crowther's work lies in her fascination with Nonsense poetry. In 'A Poet's Sense of Non-sense', which began as a series of talks for the universities of Oxford and Chichester, Crowther explores the origins and employment of her non-human, nonexistent creature, the thike, in her second collection, *The Clockwork Gift* (Shearsman, 2009). This exploration leads to a dis-cussion of the array of techniques Nonsense poems employ to diverse ends. One early remark enlarges the sense of what Nonsense poetry brings to Crowther's poetics: 'poetry can convey meaning through less than rational means'. 'Less than rational' may include such features of Nonsense poetry as the use of number, playful neologisms and invented beings, and can also include, as the body of Crowther's work indicates, sound-led passages, unexpected uses of the page and enjambment.

Syllabics is the last key agent in Crowther's poetics. As a PhD student at Kingston University, she sought a particular line to use throughout her creative thesis of grandmother poems, as she recounts in 'The Resurrected Line: Periodicity and the Grandmother Poem'. Such a line can suggest the lineage between grandmother forebears and descendant poets, for one. After encountering a hexameter line in Lee Harwood's 'African Violets', Crowther supposes she has found a line with the necessary flexibility and power for her purpose. Yet in extended practice, she discovers the hexameter is too unfamiliar for her to use effectively and gravitates toward syllabics, where she can establish a new shape for line and stanza for each new poem while also setting a pattern to which the rest of the poem adheres. Her later essay, 'Confessing to Syllabics', explores her attraction to the form while surveying the use of it in English-language poetry.

---

[1] Adrienne Raphel explains Forrest-Thomson's image-complexes as 'images built in the tension between expressions created in language and the external world' while Forrest-Thomson regards bad naturalisation as 'blindness to the complexity of those non-meaningful features which differentiate poetry from everyday language and make it something other than an external thematic statement about an already-known world' (p.36).

While she concedes that syllabics' strictures lack wide appeal, Crowther explains how they have proved enabling in her own practice.

The inclusion of reviews in this book exhibits Crowther's commitment to pluralism in poetry, taking in poets as diverse as Jean 'Binta' Breeze, Denise Riley, and Michael Symmons Roberts. Equally interesting, I find, the reviews admit room for affect within a critical response. This inclusion of the personal appears sparingly in the essays, as when 'On the Fall in Lorine Niedecker's Poetry' interweaves Crowther's visit to Wisconsin and consideration of Niedecker's life story with an appreciative analysis of several poems. In brief remarks, the reviews permit more admissions of affect. In discussing Joanne Limburg's *The Autistic Alice* and what it is to feel different to one's family members, Crowther writes, in an irrepressible aside, 'Different feelings can be embarrassing or guilt-inducing (though why should they be?)'. While such interjections may highlight a reviewer's subjectivity, they also accommodate the author's emotional response to a text. A similar moment occurs early in Crowther's review of Denise Riley's *Say Something Back,* when she relates that she 'gave in and cried' at a particular passage about the death of the poet-speaker's son. Such acknowledgment of affect importantly recognises the subjectivity of a review as well as our embodied engagement with texts.

The last section of this book comprises interviews I conducted with Crowther about each of her books in turn, which we started with this volume's inception in 2020. These interviews pick up on the central threads in Crowther's poetics as well as her engagement with publishing, critical reception, and her own development. They help elucidate her poetics as well as her writing practice and individual poems. It is my hope that this selection of essays, reviews, and interviews will give fellow admirers of Crowther's work a fuller appreciation of it. Certainly, my years working with her on this book have afforded me great insight and recognition of the compelling intelligence and originality of this body of work.

CARRIE ETTER

REFERENCES

Crowther, C. (2007) *Stretch of Closures*. Exeter: Shearsman Books.

Forrest-Thomson, V. (2016) *Poetic Artifice: A Theory of Twentieth-Century Poetry*. Edited by Farmer, G. Bristol: Shearsman Books.

Raphel, A. (n.d.) 'The Rise of Veronica Forrest-Thomson', The Poetry Foundation. Available at: https://www.poetryfoundation.org/articles/142033/the-rise-of-veronica-forrest-thomson (Accessed: 4 March 2024).

I.

Essays and Reviews

On the Fall in Lorine Niedecker's Poetry

During the summer of 1998, I stayed with friends in Wisconsin. I asked which poets came from Wisconsin, and my friends named two: Ella Wheeler Wilcox (1850–1915), well-known for the lines 'You are nearer God's heart in a garden / than anywhere else on earth' and Lorine Niedecker (1903–1970). While Wilcox was hugely famous in her lifetime, Niedecker was not, though Niedecker now has her own room at Hoard Historical Museum in Fort Atkinson, her hometown. Wilcox's poetics are late Victorian, lush and romantic, while Niedecker's are modernist and tightly clipped. Wilcox wrote poetry and novels to earn her living, and Niedecker wrote about a working life; she lived among working people, saw herself as a worker, and saw writing poems as work (CP, p.90):

> Grandfather
>   advised me:
>   Learn a trade
>
> I learned
>   to sit at desk
>   and condense
>
> No layoff
>   from this
>   condensery

Such spareness is typical of Niedecker's style. Economy was, from the start of her writing career, a notable quality of her writing. She called it 'condensing,' perhaps referring to Ezra Pound's dictum, 'dichten= condensare' (p.36). Short lines generally and often repeatedly halt the pace and can make a line more exact; for example, though an un-articled noun – 'to sit at desk' – sounds unaccountably strange, such an absence within a very short line focuses attention on every word present, noun, verb and preposition.

    While resident in Wisconsin for most of her life, Niedecker built relationships with distant poets via postal correspondence and through their occasional long journeys to Fort Atkinson to see her. In becoming an exemplary modernist poet, she was supported by such well-known

poets as Louis Zukofsky and Basil Bunting. Zukofsky became a friend for
life and advised her on her poems regularly. Bunting, a British modernist,
discovered Niedecker through Zukofsky and visited her in Fort Atkinson,
commenting that 'she was the most important woman poet America has
yet produced' (p.163).

Niedecker began writing in her teens and had poems published
in her twenties in *Poetry* magazine, edited then by Harriet Monroe.
Niedecker wrote to Zukofsky after reading the 1931 issue of *Poetry*,
which was devoted to Zukofsky and his friends, known from then on as
Objectivists. He responded, and she stayed with him for a while in New
York. They had a brief romantic relationship and maintained a lifelong
friendship, mostly through a regular exchange of letters. She wrote several
poems about Zukofsky's son, Paul, such as this one (CP, p.44):

> Paul
>   when the leaves
>   fall
>
> from their stems
>   that lie thick
>   on the walk
>
> in the light
>   of the full note
>   the moon
>
> playing
>   to leaves
>   when they leave
>
> the little
>   thin things
>   Paul

Frailty – the moon is full but 'little / thin things' are being lost, are leaving
– permeates the poem, which is one of a set of fifty called 'For Paul'
written between 1949, when Paul was six, and 1953. This poem has no
title (I'll call it 'Paul' for this essay), a common absence in Niedecker's
work. Typically, Niedecker puts a space or absence above the poem rather

than a title. Here, the absence adds to the sense of loss in general, loss exemplified in the first stanza as leaves. In the absence of a title, the first line is foregrounded, and it is simply a name, Paul. It's moving to think of the complexity of feelings Niedecker must have had for this child, especially since it is believed (see Perloff, in Penberthy 1996, p.159), that, after her romance with Zukofsky, she had an abortion (p.4). Leaves fall, in this poem, and appear as 'little / thin / things.' The final stanza runs 'the little / thin things' together with 'Paul' so leaves can be read as children, and, of course, the word 'leaves' carries the sense of going away.

The poem 'Paul' is an exemplar of absence within the tight space of a short poem; the stem – the poem itself – is bare. There is no punctuation apart from the one capital letter, P for Paul, giving the name a little emphasis. In the poem, staggered lines and the lack of stops and commas suggest the weightlessness of leaves (words) falling. The name, Paul, appears to the left at the very top but to the right at the end. Naming the boy, first and last, also summons him, peremptorily. The subsequent description of falling leaves gives a metaphorical description of him, of his life and the loss of his childhood, whether through age or death. This identification of Paul as lost leaf enlarges the metaphoric scope of the poem. More than one leaf falls in the poem. The lost leaves are plural in the final stanza: 'the little / thin things'. The stanzas are all 'little thin things', short lines, repeating three-line stepped stanzas. Words echo and repeat, 'leaves ... leave', 'lie ... light', 'thin things', "Paul ... fall". The repetitions create a picture of a pile of leaves, despite the bare visual quality of the poem. Paul, the fragile 'thin thing' is standing on a heap of leaves; such piles appear in fairy tales perhaps as a place to sleep or a burial mound for children. Perhaps Niedecker wishes to indicate the fragility of children; throughout Niedecker's minimal words and stark lines in this poem, the voice and mood are gentle, careful, almost as if worried about the child falling.

The first verse of the poem suggests loss. It situates Paul in autumn, a time often associated with loss:

> Paul
>   when the leaves
>   fall

Yet in the second verse, the leaves don't fall from the obvious tree, but from already felled branches:

> from their stems
>   that lie thick
>   on the walk

The walk may refer to a sidewalk or an active walk. The thickness suggests a pile or the solidity of the stems. If the metaphor of leaf-child holds, while only a frail suggestion itself in this poem, then a parent is a stem, and that parent has died, being now part of the pile of stems 'thick / on the walk'. Indeed, a parent does not survive the loss of a child in the full sense of survival, though a parent might survive just as trees flourish in subsequent springs.

The third verse continues into night:

> in the light
>   of the full note
>   the moon

It is a moonlit night, and trees make this a magical place; the sensation is of a leafy landscape or cityscape in autumn. There is music: the 'full note'. The moon is not a pale substitute for the sun – it has a full note of its own. This could be an obscure reference to femaleness, the source of mothering. When the sun, life, has gone, the moon, the potential mother, rises.

Niedecker used the word 'playing' to make it clear that Paul was learning to play the violin. Rachel Blau DuPlessis, describing Paul as 'Zukofsky's prodigious young son Paul (the well-known violinist to whom Niedecker wrote "musical" offerings)', added that he was a person who 'figures in Niedecker's imagination as a sibling artist, or even as an imaginary son, for the complexities of affiliation, some filial piety, some love longing carefully set aside' (p.97).

In the fourth stanza, the musical theme continues:

> playing
>   to leaves
>   when they leave

The moon plays, as Paul did in real life, as a violinist and in the sense of a child's recreation. Both moon and Paul lament dead leaves as they leave – a beautiful use of 'leave' in the senses of giving and falling. Now the voice begins to keen:

> the little
>   thin things
>   Paul

The rhythm of the words is soft enough almost to stroke the little, thin, dead leaves, contributes to the evocation of Paul here. The poem addresses him as he retains the littleness and thinness of a dead leaf. While this sadness could spoil the poem with sentimentality, with the shift of focus to the subject of the poem, the poem completes without a collapse – not often true of a Niedecker poem, which uses such devices as collapse, voice change, and irony to convey reality without sentimentality.

Syntactically, the poem is also interesting as it never completes the sentence it promises. Niedecker wrote to Cid Corman in 1962: 'You… have thrown off the shackles of the sentence and the wide melody. For me, the sentence lies in wait – all those prepositions and connectives – like an early spring flood' (Faranda, p.33). There are prepositions and connectives here, but the sentence almost stutters to its halt on the last line; Paul's name supports, rather than concludes it.

I see the riches of Objectivism and Imagist influences in 'Paul': hard pictures, condensed, stacking up ideas and images blow after blow, lightning dashes between heart and head. 'Paul' is an early poem on Niedecker's way to her own definition of how she wanted her poems to be. Towards the end of her life, she wrote to Gail Roub (Penberthy, 1996, p.86):

> Much taken up with hope to define a way of writing poetry which is not Imagist nor Objectivist fundamentally nor Surrealism alone – reflective maybe. The basis is direct and clear – what has been seen or heard etc but something gets us, overlays all that to a state of consciousness… modern poetry and old poetry if it is good proceeds not from one point to the next linearly but in a circle. The tone of the thing. And awareness of everything influencing everything… I used to feel I was goofing off unless I held only to the hard, clear image, the thing you could put your hand on but now I dare do this reflection.

Here Niedecker is moving away from categories she held important
at an earlier stage and developing her own category: reflective poetry.
Like the seasons, so important in 'Paul', she emphasises the circularity
of good poetry and of 'everything influencing everything.' In 'Paul', one
can almost see words that are not there but that show its possible meanings: moon/mourn, leaves/lives, lie/die, thin/then, Paul/caul, thick/sick.
It's possible to replace key words to show the discourse under the images:

> Paul
>   when the lives
>   fall
>
> from their stems
>   that lie sick
>   on the stalks
>
> in the light
>   of the ill note
>   we mourn
>
> saying
>   to lives
>   when they leave
>
> the literal
>   think things
>   Paul

Compare 'Paul' with 'Fall', one part of 'Traces of Living Things', a poem
written many years later (pp.113, 114):

> We must pull
> the curtains —
> we haven't any
> leaves
>
> *
>
> Unsurpassed in beauty
> this autumn day

[…]

High class human
got no illumine

how a ten cent plant
winds aslant

around a post

This poem is divided into sections; 'Fall', a section head, reflects the
several other parts of this long poem, hinting at the many meanings of
fall. It conjures human guilt from natural imagery, as in 'Human bean /
and love-over-the-fence' (p.114), an allusion to sexual betrayal. The tone
is edgy and defensive: 'I'm a fool / can't take it cool' (p.114). Whereas
the voice in 'Paul' is willing to be sad, this voice can't accept life calmly:
'can't take it cool'. The best (or politically worst) people 'got no illumine',
natural growth ('bean') is over the fence, away from home in someone
else's backyard, and distortions are manifest in the choppy structure
– lines are shorter, from one word to five words, lines are positioned
differently from stanza to stanza, ranged left or stepped, stanza length
varies from four to three to two (though the last stanza reverts to three).
The short stanza, 'Fall', suggests the result of loss or lack: 'we haven't any /
leaves'.

There are many other instances of the leaf metaphor in Niedecker's
work. Loosely, leaves often seem to suggest children and love and grow on
trees that may represent men and sex. This stanza from 'Paean to Place'
could almost be an addition to 'Paul':

To be counted on:
    new leaves
        new dead
leaves

It may be because she cuts so much, restricts her picture so much, that
Niedecker's spare poetry conveys pain so well. Niedecker married for a
second time late in her life (her first marriage had been brief) and wrote
in 1967 (BC, no pagination):

I married

in the world's black night
for warmth
                if not repose.
                At the close—
someone.

I hid with him
from the long range guns.
                We lay leg
                in the cupboard, head
        in closet.

She sent this poem to her friend Cid Corman saying it was 'rather spon-
taneous from folk conversation and I suppose some of my own dark
forebodings. We should be true to our subconscious? Sorry it is another I
poem. My god I must try to get away from that' (Faranda, p.129).

'Paean to Place', the first poem I read by Niedecker, refers to Black
Hawk Island, a small peninsula near Fort Atkinson. Niedecker's father
owned some property there as well as a fishing business. There were problems: her father had an affair with a neighbour, and Niedecker's mother
became deaf. As a consequence of her mother's deafness, Niedecker grew
unusually aware of sound. The family lived on the banks of Lake Kosh-
konong, close to the water, which flooded often, an area noisy with birds.
It is also, I found, a stunning place visually. Though Niedecker grew blind
in later life, her poetry includes precise descriptions of the visual features
as well as the sounds of Black Hawk Island (CP, pp.14, 17):

Fish
    fowl
        flood
    Water lily mud
My life

in the leaves and on water

[…]

I was the solitary plover
a pencil
   for a wing-bone

These lines, as in 'Paul', look artless, but they are patterned with alliteration and assonance. Niedecker always handles space on the page carefully: there are indents like inlets in the stanzas, the lines ripple in and return to the left-hand margin, and there is a bird-like quality to the last stanza.

Underneath her verbal and formal ingenuity, a childlike rhythm often flows. It is present in these lines, for example: 'My mother and I / born / in swale and swamp and sworn' (p.14). Niedecker uses a nursery rhyme rhythm here and, elsewhere, simple two-beat lines and childhood expressions in many poems. Since my trip to Fort Atkinson, I can picture Niedecker as a child; she wrote to Kenneth Cox that 'I feel as tho I spent my childhood outdoors' (Dent, p.36). She wrote about and for Paul, but also for the child who never left home.

REFERENCES

Bunting, B. (1985) '"Brief Words Are Hard To Find": Basil Bunting & Lorine Niedecker', *Conjunctions,* 8, pp.159-164. Available at: https://www.jstor.org/stable/24514680 (Accessed: 22 February 2024).

Dent, P. (1983) 'Lorine Niedecker: Extracts from Letters to Kenneth Cox' in *The Full Note: Lorine Niedecker.* Budleigh Salterton: Interim Press.

DuPlessis, R.B. (1992) 'Lorine Niedecker, the Anonymous: Gender, Class, Genre and Resistances', *The Kenyon Review,* New Series 14 (2), pp.96-116. Available at: https://www.jstor.org/stable/4336668 (accessed 22 February 2024).

Faranda, L.P. (1986) *"Between Your House and Mine": The Letters of Lorine Niedecker to Cid Corman 1960 to 1970.* Durham: Duke University Press.

Niedecker, L. (1970) *My Life By Water. Collected Poems 1936–1968.* London: Fulcrum Press. [CP in the text]

Niedecker, L. (1976) *Blue Chicory.* Edited by Corman, C. New Rochelle, NY: The Elizabeth Press. [BC in the text]

Penberthy, J. (1996) (ed.) *Lorine Niedecker Woman and Poet.* Orono, ME: National Poetry Foundation.

Penberthy, J. (2005) *Niedecker and the Correspondence with Zukofsky, 1931–1970.* Cambridge: Cambridge University Press.

Pound, E. (1963) *ABC of Reading.* London: Faber and Faber.

The Resurrected Line:
Periodicity and the Grandmother Poem

When I undertook a PhD in creative writing, producing a creative thesis consisting of an essay and a sequence of poems about grandmotherhood, one of my earliest ideas was that I might use one type of line in all the poems. This possibility felt radical as I usually let each single poem dictate its own approach to the line. As Pound said, even 'Homer did not start by thinking which of the sixty-four permitted formulae was to be used in his next verse' (p.204). Many contemporary poets would agree. Rodney Pybus says, 'I like the challenge of searching for a new form each time, finding a way out of silence' (p.378). Yet I wanted to focus on the line, and line is essential to the concept and the reality of grandmotherhood, a term redolent of genealogy. I began to think about grandmotherhood as a metaphor for a poet's lineage.

Grandmother poems are written for many reasons, and there is one common effect: the grandmother can be read as the figure of a writer. The writer creates a poem; if it is read many years hence by a poet, the reader looks back at the older or perhaps deceased writer as a child looks back at a grandmother, as if that figure were an ancestor in a line of heritage, which could include writing poetry or even particular forms of it. The grandmother, the ancestral poet in this metaphor, represents beginnings, of a line, of a poet, of the poet who considers the origins of her poetics. Sarah Vap differentiates the relationship between herself and her literary forebears, grandfather as opposed to grandmother, in her exploration of the line: 'I think of our grandparent poets. Whitman, the horizontal line I inherited, opened his arms wide to hold the whole body of world. / / Dickinson, her vertical axis that is the basis of my own, opened to the heavens above and the heavens below' (p.244). Grandfather is grounded and very much of this life whereas Vap's female forebear, this quote seems to suggest, is ethereal, otherworldly, a before- and afterlife. What might be the particular function of a grandmother, then, in the life of a poet, female or male, today, and how can a particular use of the line show it? Peter Reading suggests the function of a 'gran' in his two-line grandmother poem: 'Grans are bewildered by post-Coronation disintegration – / offspring of offspring of *their* offspring infest and despoil' (p.39). This poem is a couplet, two lines that depict, simply, before and after. A feminist might note a hint of Eve's curse here in the emphasis on 'their' offspring. Is the infestation and despoliation all, in fact, Gran's fault?

This periodicity of the couplet, its before and after, the lost and found of the line, its end and its resurrection, succinctly suggests the function of the line in any poem: a line dying and a line being born, at regular intervals. As I read grandmother poems and wrote my own, I found that in grandmother poems written by other poets over the past thirty-plus years, the grandmother figure often comes to represent the periodicity of losing, finding, and again forgetting the work of female poets: many excellent female poets were famous in their own era, but are not known now. They may be rediscovered by contemporary writers who can then share them with readers as Robert Galbraith (J.K. Rowling) has done in the crime novel, *The Ink Black Heart* (2022), quoting as chapter epigraphs Letitia Elizabeth Landon, Felicia Hemans and Jean Ingelow as well as poets whose names are still well known, Emily Dickinson, Elizabeth Barrett Browning and Christina Rossetti. From the 1970s onward, many Anglophone female poets have written about the experience of writing alongside a canon that does not represent their work; some have found the grandmother a useful trope to explore this exclusion.

The periodicity inherent in the form of poetry, lines and stanzas beginning, ending and recurring, is reflected in the short lives of most poems and, of course, in the short lives of human beings. The poem's most basic period or unit is the line. Emily Grosholz defines periodicity as (2005, pp.260-261)

> symmetry in time. When people take up periodicity mindfully, and turn it into departure and return, regret and anticipation, the representations they use often turn periodicity back to spatial symmetry. We do this on the round faces of our clocks that superimpose midnight on midday... Symmetry that stands for periodicity is also depicted on the printed page in the lineation of a poem....

'Symmetry in time' suggests a future effect could be a past reality, so there are future possibilities for the poem, and such possibilities include a heritage. In a similar way, the grandmother, possibly herself a poet, may generate a future poet. Every poet has her human beginning in the family line and her beginning as a poet in her foremother-poets. This generation of line seems to me similar to the offering that a line makes to a poem: a regular beginning of the organisation of ideas and sounds. There too in each line is its ending, a regular discontinuing and, unsurprisingly then, grandmother poems often address discontinuity, perhaps as an expression of anxiety about loss of the author's life and work.

The repeating line provides a good vehicle for the theme of regeneration; consequently, I suspected that prose poetry – defined as lineless – would be a poor choice for my grandmother poems. Geoffrey Hill's twenty-fifth Mercian hymn is a grandmother poem that may be thought of as prose. The words are spaced to occupy lines upon which Hill has decided: the poem would have the same line endings were it in a different font size. However, the poem is justified to look like prose (p.107):

> Brooding on the eightieth letter of *Fors Clavigera*,
>   I speak this in memory of my grandmother, whose
>   childhood and prime womanhood were spent in the
>   nailer's darg.

Note, if these are lines, Hill's use of enjambment. Enjambment, turning the line without finishing it grammatically and thus extending the meaning into the following line, seems to show a line that wants to live on. The second line, ending on the pronoun 'whose', carries the thought forward without stopping grammatically. That pronoun emphasises the grandmother to whom it applies even while indicating that there are particularly interesting aspects of her – 'childhood' and 'prime womanhood' – to which the poet wants to draw attention. The third line, by ending on 'the' and forcing a pause, holds off naming 'nailer's darg', a striking, presumably unexpected phrase. Notwithstanding enjambment, in the need to repeat and in the nature of periodicity, lines in a poem die, every one. I feel there is an elegiac quality to the notion of the poetic line that prose doesn't have. Hill's stanza above is an example of both sorts of line ending: it begins with a resounding line that has an emphatic ending and follows with lines that read as prose, with endings that occur rather more quickly and casually than if traditionally lineated.

The traditional poetic line lies flat across the page and dies, so to speak, before it reaches the right hand margin. A dead grandmother might be supposed to lie in such a horizontal fashion. William Watkin writes (pp.86-87):

> As the line is in the poem so the body is in death. ... When the line lies down, the body becomes a corpse, but when the line rises up, the corpse becomes a living form once more. ... the poetic line both lies down on the page but, through the semiotics of the line break, also does not lie down but aspires upwards towards spiritual ascendancy and emotional sublimation.

The line not only dies, but is reborn in time over and over again.

Becoming aware that there are multiple beginnings spiritually and emotionally on the page enhanced the importance of the first line of any grandmother poem I might write. I conjectured that the first line of a grandmother poem could, perhaps should, reflect the pre-existence of a grandmother. I began to write such lines as 'Take note of my grandmother's white veil' (Crowther, 2009) in the poet's voice and 'Where are they now, the transparent walkways' in the voice of a narrating grandmother (Crowther, 2009). I also wondered whether occasionally to allow the first line of some of my grandmother poems to take the position of title, to suggest subliminally that first lines are foremothers to the ensuing poem. Additionally, I considered the role of the last line; surely that must be important, too. 'Arraheids', a grandmother poem by Kathleen Jamie, presents the last line, 'whae do you think ye are', as an interrogation of its own gendered metaphor: ancient arrowheads. The poem describes the flint arrowheads in museum cases and museum visitors' curiosity about their own prehistory. 'Bewaur', the poet says: if you look too hard you will find these weapons are 'the hard tongues o' grannies' (Jamie, 2002, p.137). Thus, Jamie suggests, our prehistory shows that women have weapons, and even the misogynist trope of a woman's chattering tongue, imaged in the poem as an arrowhead, is, in fact, a phallic image for grandmother; grannies' tongues are tough, whatever they may be talking about, and that grandmotherly discourse, in my view, includes poetry.

Between these two positions, first and last line, grandmother poems often appear to be little boxes, rather coffin-like, while, of course, regularly breaking out of the box. Early in 'Divination by Hair', Ruth Fainlight uses a traditional iambic pentameter to describe the granny stereotype. Later in the poem, the line breaks down under the weight of the speaker's anxiety. These lines from the beginning and end of the poem show the striking formal contrast (Fainlight, 1987, p.72):

If only it could happen overnight:
one morning I would wake transformed into
that dignified wise matron of my dreams
matured at last to grace (though I make her sound
like the grandmother on a birthday card...

            days   mirror
                    dozen hairs   white
        dubious   purpose
    despising
            ideal   stubbornly...

This linguistic breakdown questions a grandmother's role. The page is full of gaps, suggesting that the grandparent's understanding of how to be 'ideal', and what the 'purpose' of such a role is, fluctuates.

A 'dignified wise matron' is identified as one with a grandchild here, simply by using the word 'grandmother'. The relationship between grandchild and grandmother bears a haunting sense of responsibility, of care and, especially for grandmother, a desire to be wiser than she may be. This wish is hard to achieve in those cases where a grandmother poem is a dialogue between two people who may not even know each other yet are interdependent for identity and even existence.

In a grandmother poem called 'Arioso Dolente', Anne Stevenson writes: 'Ours is the breath on which the past depends' (2004, p.318). Not only does a contemporary poet gain confidence, knowledge and a sense of entitlement from a grandmother, some poets act on behalf of the grandmother, resurrecting long forgotten names and texts. Josephine Balmer, for example, has published a collection of her translations of female poets from ancient Greece who have been overlooked for centuries (*Classical Women Poets*, Bloodaxe, 1996). The feminist reader may notice how many of these poems go beyond ageing and death to the loss of poetry, a realm where the poet can address the grandmother. A grandmother poem raises the possibility that we are not separate from our ancestors, through bloodline or poetic line, and that this once ordinary biological mother could also become a mother of future writers. For my purposes, lineation, like every other tool of poetics, should try to express the unusual and specific nature of the relationship between poet and forerunners. As Eavan Boland says about syntax in a grandmother poem called 'Lava Cameo', it's 'a structure extrinsic to meaning which uncovers / the inner secret of it' (1995, p.196). Line is also both a structure and an element in the poem's larger structure; its formation is part of the delivery of a poem's meanings. The lineation of a poem designedly creates, enhances, or simply affects meaning; the habits of lineation, how to use the line and when to use it, draw on poetic customs laid down through centuries.

Lee Harwood's grandmother poem 'African Violets' gave me the idea for a line that could underpin my own collection of grandmother poems, later to become *The Clockwork Gift* (Crowther, 2009). While not all grandmother poems are about real-life grandmothers, 'African Violets' is an elegy for his own paternal grandmother, Pansy Harwood. She is also the dedicatee of the *Collected Poems* in which it appears. Even so, throughout the poem, Harwood draws our attention to his conviction that poetry is fiction, and I want to look at the poem in this light.

'African Violets' uses lines of varying lengths, syllable counts and stresses. The story of this particular poem is simple: a man's grandmother dies, he misses her and grieves. In a reflection of this loss, the lines are regularly truncated throughout the poem, some float in space (like lost souls?), and holes appear amid words. The first stanza offers three long lines, followed by the recognisable voice of a mourning grandson, 'tears in my eyes' (Harwood, p.432). The language of the phrase, 'pages of words creating old routines', suggests a grandmother located in a past era. The words relate to a woman who lived through an earlier era and spoke a different language from her grandson, as we see when she uses the phrases 'a real heart-breaker' and 'with all a lovely generosity'.

In line 12, the speaker asks the grandmother a direct question and answers it for her: 'And you gave me?   everything I know'. Such questioning is a recurring device in Harwood's poems and a pivotal point in this poem. It would seem he wants to stave off his full belief in the gifts from his relationship with his grandmother, and to suggest we cannot, honestly, say we understand any relationship, being the complex beings that we are. The answer, 'everything I know', a disarming cliché, is reminiscent of countless poems to be found on websites dedicated to grandmothers. I see that answer as a conflation of poetry with the oral storytelling associated with grandmothers, an association emphasised by Marina Warner, among others (1995). Whatever Pansy told the young Harwood, he claims that as his knowledge. A contemporary poet such as Harwood will, of course, add to the knowledge handed down by his poetic forebear, replace it even, as over the centuries poets use forms and stories handed down by generations of predecessors.

The lines following the speaker's question to his grandmother in 'African Violets' defend Harwood's own position as a younger poet who must find a new poetic approach: the 'old routines / I systematically smash all those pretty pictures, / they won't do anymore' (p.432). Despite the casting off of 'old routines', the narrator suggests that the family line and, metaphorically, the poetic influence of an ancestor, will not be lost, as 'your blood continues to flow in me / no matter what I might say...' (Harwood, p.433).

If the grandmother is the speaker's educator, in the domestic idyll of 'African Violets' he is her help-meet as housekeeper. The poem is full of images that suggest home is handed down through generations: 'Flags stream from the tops of the silver pyramids', 'jasmin bower', 'the comfort your home was / ...almost another world', 'the rich world about'. Harwood describes aspects of his grandmother's domestic space – her house (p.433):

Yet it seems almost another world –
building rabbit hutches on winter evenings
in your living room, sawdust and
wood shavings on the worn carpet, easily cleaned.
A house that was lived in, not exhibited.

The indoor space and accoutrements of home have been associated with women for centuries, and Harwood's poem associates a grandmother with 'home', engaging with her physical 'objects'. Harwood interprets 'home' in a wider social context, beginning and ending the poem with references to flags, those indicators of homeland power. The poem suggests art and the world are at odds with each other in the second and third lines: 'the world / Chopin fights his way through'.

The association of 'house' with a grandmother occurs in poems from other cultures than British. Pilar Adón, a Spanish poet, describes a grandmother at length in her poem 'Stigma' and concludes in a final couplet: 'She loved her house, my grandma. / It's yours for 30,000 euros' (p.7). I read this as Adón suggesting the disposal of what a grandmother loved is inevitable and transactional, and what she loved has a price. Yet the preceding lines in Adón's poem evoke the influence and strength of this grandmother just as acutely Harwood does:

> I never saw her cry, my grandmother.
> Her womb came out of her vagina,
> she healed herself with lemon…
> She cut the nails of newborn girls
> so they'd sing true like her.

Defined by her ability to endure without tears, exposed to her granddaughter as progenitor by her womb, this grandmother can heal herself and has the power to enable baby girls to sing as she does.

Harwood recognises just such a physical closeness in his relationship with Pansy ('My blood is your blood', p.432) as he describes himself happily joining his grandmother in (male-associated) activities such as building with wood, as well as such (female-associated) activities as bottling food, transcending gendered relationships (p.433):

> And all those other evenings, summer or winter,
> spent pickling onions, or bottling fruit,
> or wrapping boxes of apples for store,
> or stringing onions to hang in the shed
>   above the sacked potatoes…

The poem uses numerous images of containment: pyramids, pot, hospital room, home, living room, house, bottling, boxes, shed, room and, in the end, the poem contains or houses the grandmother. The periodicity of departing and returning lines, opening and closing of stanzas, the spatial symmetry of black text superimposing on white space, also frame the grandmother inside the poem's body since, for the reader, there will be no other contact with the grandmother presented to us. Just as grandchildren feel grandmothers belong to them, as Harwood's narrator claims his grandmother and loses her in his eulogy, so younger women poets read the work of past female poets, realise their debt and gain a sense of carrying on a tradition of writing poetry, a validating process for a new writer.

Similarly, a granddaughter poet validates and, in some cases, rediscovers her dead poet mentors, bringing a satisfying circularity to this process. Harwood's poem itself feels circular. The first three lines are one of only two tercets in the poem. It describes a funeral, it seems, with flags, flowers and music, followed by a two-line description of how 'that emptiness' feels. The narrator has 'tears in [his] eyes'. A tercet followed by two lines ends the poem, again with flags and 'the rich world about' despite the narrator being inside the room. Now, after the emotional journey of the poem, the narrator does not mention the 'emptiness' of the earlier passage, but sees his grandmother: 'I see you again and again sat there'. Thus the opening and closing lines suggest a grandson coming to terms with his loss. This formal boxing of a psychological drama inside a story, the placing of the story inside a poem as well as, or perhaps rather than, the real world, all allow the poet to go beyond strict autobiography, as such conversational poems are sometimes assumed to be. Indeed, the narrator says that both he and his grandmother are 'natural liars…turning facts to meet the story…' (p.433). Harwood says in an interview (2003):

> And there's that thing about writing … which is like making a toy theatre, which is the pleasure of constructing this story, the story matters but also being able to pull in all these questions that say: "well hang on do you really believe that?" Or is this really going on? It takes it far beyond the story, which is a bit like having stuff going on in the street outside the scene.

Reading 'African Violets', I believe the story is also 'really going on' beyond the poem, especially when Harwood refers to both himself and his grandmother being 'natural liars …easy with the "truth"' (p.432). The lines work as narrative threads, sewing together explorations of ideas and images, a method that allows movement in and out of the story to question the poet's own integrity: 'pages of words creating old routines'… won't do anymore'; 'we both… were, are natural liars / easy with the "truth"'.

The last line sums up the periodicity of a grandmother's loss: 'I see you again and again sat there'. But who is sitting there? Is the grandmother listening to his poem? Or is the narrator 'sat there', seeing her? The space both conjures the empty chair and suggests that the distress of loss induces speechlessness. There are five beats in the line of words, in my view an iamb, two anapests and two spondees. There is also a beat of silence in the large gap between the second 'again' and 'sat there', the largest in-line space in the poem. The fiction we create around our relationships, including that with a grandmother, is contained in this line – that, though her chair is empty, and there is a space in the place where we last met her, nevertheless we can 'see' her 'again and again' beyond the painful hole in our life, and that she therefore has not gone entirely. Death cannot cause complete absence. The line allows the grandson's emotion to resonate with the possibility of her continuing presence.

It seems to me that this line could contain six stresses, with the space holding one beat and that beat taking a stress: 'I **see** you a**gain** and a**gain** sat **there**'. This line gave me the idea that perhaps iambic hexameter could work well for my grandmother sequence. It is long enough to break inside in varying places; it can stretch to suggest the distance between grandmother and grandchild. The hexameter is an ancient line, the oldest Greek verse, and has also been at the heart of many creative developments in poetics; Reading's couplet begins with a dactylic hexameter. No doubt the hexameter could convey the idea of the grandmother as a foremother for her granddaughter and a grandson's patriarchal construction of a muse in the grandmother. Yet could it suggest what I felt personally as the beyond-ordinary situation of a living grandmother – that just when a woman is becoming aware of her own death, moving back within her self and out of relationships, out of the community, her grown up children are expanding the community with their own children and pressing her into childcare? At the end of her life, she is absorbed and taken into the future by a child she has had no biological part in conceiving. I started to write grandmother poems using an iambic hexameter line.

Before long, though, it became obvious that I couldn't write well to an unfamiliar rhythm. I must have a granny line that is the grandmother I made of her, my fictional sound, my personal version of the practice I have inherited. Nonetheless, some hexameter lines remain scattered through the poems in *The Clockwork Gift*. These were not acknowledgments of past forms, but of the extra weight the past carries for a poet who is reading extensively and finding her own bearings within her tradition. In one poem in *The Clockwork Gift*, I used the hexameter more successfully (p.20):

Woman, Probably One of the Fates
'This is one of a number of representations of hideously ugly old
women by the same hand...' Exhibit note, National Gallery of
Scotland, Edinburgh

When wrinkles etch so deeply they lattice neck
and muzzle forehead, skin takes over,

makes a fabric of old stone. What I see
in my inner arm when it's bare and bent, raising a glass,

is Fate holding her drapery. It's what I expect
though bones would be more likely. Here is an outstanding
          breastbone.

When I wrote this poem, the rhythm felt right for a description of
age, for the depiction of Fate. Did I hear the sound of a line formed of
ancient metrical beats? Yet the penultimate line, with a sudden caesura,
throws down a challenge to its own long metrical expectation: 'skin is
resistance'. Skin, covering the body, could be seen as an image of a poem's
lines holding the beat and meaning inside itself. I saw for myself why the
hexameter's sixth foot is not usual for English-language poetry and, while
that abnormality fascinated and challenged me, I could not continue
with it.

I gave up on hexameters and have rarely written them since; I
primarily used varying lines for *The Clockwork Gift*. That collection has
many grandmother poems, and I explored the experiences of historical as
well as contemporary grandmothers throughout it. Yet, even as I wrote
that collection, I was not comfortable with the degree of range that free
verse gives, and I soon turned to syllabics, a pattern established through
counting the syllables in a line or stanza and repeating that count to
make a pattern. This method of organising a poem has a huge variety
of numeric possibilities and can adjust to the needs of different poems.
Once the syllabic structure of a poem is set, its line is implacable, as grandmotherhood is, once a daughter gives birth. I say implacable because I
found the creation of my own grandmotherhood, a creation made by my
daughters giving birth in their own time for their own reasons, a shock.
The announcement is of a pregnancy; what happens to a grandmother
is a birth and it must be gone through. The syllabic line, once its pattern
is established, seemed to me to have that quality of non-emotional non-
adjustable delivery. In subsequent collections I have made increasing use
of syllabics.

I believe that, though the poetic line of my time is the line that
Harwood uses, an ever-changing line within a poem with no regular beat,
no expectation put on the line to repeat, I am now most comfortable
with the syllabic line. This is the line that counts, that respects what has
gone before in the poem, that sets a precedent as it opens the poem and
acknowledges its past as it finishes. In this way, the syllabically controlled
line presents an ongoing repetition just as a woman who creates will have
grandchildren; it is not her choice. She must contend with line's pattern,

a pattern that is strictly practical. The line's pattern is a matter of poetic practice too; in my case a syllabic draft is integrated into the evolution of each poem, so a syllabic pattern has become part of my ongoing process.

A syllabic line is representative of my time as a poet but it is not the line of my time; it is the line of a culture whose language offers syllables. The use of English-language syllabics to give poetic form is often disliked, is not widely used, and may be invisible to the reader, but it persists. If syllabic poetry is simply a throwing off of outdated approaches, of metre and rhythm, perhaps it is also the hardest duty of a new poet and a new grandmother, as I was when I began to explore the grandmother poem. When I read my foremothers' work, I see how many of them influenced contemporary poetics and how many of them wrote when a woman was not expected to be a published poet. In the end, the grandmother line is not about a way to write, but an example of the enduring will to continue.

REFERENCES

Acheson, J. and Huk, R. (eds) (1996) *Contemporary British Poetry: Essays in Theory and Criticism*. New York, NY: State University of New York Press.

Adón, P. (2020) 'Stigma', in Dooley, T. (ed./trans.) *Ten Contemporary Spanish Women Poets*. Bristol: Shearsman Books.

Balmer, J. (1996) *Classical Women Poets*. Tarset: Bloodaxe Books.

Boland, E. (1995) *Collected Poems*. Manchester: Carcanet Press.

Crowther, C. (2009) *The Clockwork Gift*. Exeter: Shearsman Books.

Fainlight, R. (1987) *Selected Poems*. London: Hutchinson.

Galbraith, R. (2022) *The Ink Black Heart*. London: Sphere Books.

Grosholz, E. (2005) 'The Uses of Periodicity in English Verse', *Hudson Review* 58 (2), pp.259-274.

Harwood, L. (2004) *Collected Poems*. Exeter: Shearsman Books.

Harwood, L. (2003) Interviewed by Aodán McCardle on September 2 for Birkbeck College. Available at: www.bbk.ac.uk/readings/rl/harwood.html (Accessed: 15 September 2006).

Hill, G. (2013) *Broken Hierarchies: Poems 1952–2012*. Edited by Haynes, K. Oxford: Oxford University Press.

Jamie, K. (2002) *Mr and Mrs Scotland are Dead: Poems 1980–1994*. Tarset: Bloodaxe Books.

Kerrigan, J. (2004) 'Notes from the Home Front: Contemporary British Poetry', *Essays in Criticism* 54 (2), pp.103-27.

Lee, S., Colditz, G., Berkman, L., and Kawachi, I. (2003) 'Caregiving to Children and Grandchildren and Risk of Coronary Heart Disease in Women', *American Journal of Public Health,* 93 (11), pp.1933-44.

Pound, E. (1963) *ABC of Reading.* London: Faber and Faber.

Pybus, R. (1967) 'Free and Metrical Verse', in Silkin, J. (ed) *The Life of Metrical and Free Verse in Twentieth-Century Poetry.* London: Macmillan, pp.378-381.

Reading, P. (1996) *Collected Poems. 1985–1996.* Tarset: Bloodaxe Books.

Stevenson, A. (2004) *Poems 1955–2005.* Tarset: Bloodaxe Books.

Vap, S. (2011) 'Line: So We Go Away', in Roako, E., and Vander Zee, A. (eds.) *A Broken Thing: Poets on the Line.* Iowa City, IA: University of Iowa Press, pp.243-247.

Warner, M. (1995) *From the Beast to the Blonde.* London: Vintage.

Watkin, W. (2004) *On Mourning: Theories of Loss in Modern Literature.* Edinburgh: Edinburgh University Press.

Start This End

In Person: 30 Poets
filmed by Pamela Robertson-Pearce and edited by Neil Astley

The Ropes: Poems to Hold On To
edited by Sophie Hannah and John Hegley

The Ropes: Poems to Hold On To (Diamond Twig, 2008) is marketed as an anthology for adolescents, but defined firmly by Sophie Hannah, one of the two editors, as 'not a book for teenagers' (p.9). The poems appear in two sets, one written by women, the other by men, and, amusingly, the reader has to turn the book upside down to read the other section. These poems address not so much what might concern an adolescent today, though he or she might enjoy them, but what concerns an adult looking back at the experience of adolescence. Jane Holland writes in 'My school photograph' (p.37):

> You never quite believed in yourself,
> girl with the gorgeous hair
> and the V-neck jumper, sad-eyed,
> not yet sixteen.

Nostalgia ('gorgeous hair') dominates recollections of a difficult time of life ('sad-eyed, / not yet sixteen'). Alongside the poems are photos with explanatory notes from the poets, usually from when they were teenagers: 'I didn't like how skinny I was as a teenager', says Gwyneth Lewis (p.42). 'I was 14, taking nothing seriously', reflects W.N. Herbert (p.24).

Somewhat disorientating is the inclusion of a few dead poets such as Louis MacNeice and Edna St Vincent Millay. While their poems do not differ much emotionally from the others, their language varies from that of the contemporary poets. Louis MacNeice, for example, describes a young person, perhaps himself, as 'the youth whom whisky had led astray' (p.29) and, later in his poem, MacNeice inverts the more modern syntax that would put a main verb before a descriptive phrase: 'And when from Eden we take our way' (p.29). This style differs markedly from Herbert's description of cannabis intoxication: 'their half-known pals lie stoned / in rented dives' (p.25), and the anthology itself has a contemporary visual design. It is small enough to carry round and dip into, with blank spaces opposite every poem bearing a faintly printed exhortation to 'respond' when you've brooded over some of these reflections on life and love. The following lines by Moniza Alvi might warm a young adult on a cold day ('Self-belief', p.17):

> Then think of your intricate humanness,
> your holy simplicity
>
> moment by moment by moment.

I suspect that, because of its design and appearance, *The Ropes* will be bought for teenagers, but will those adolescents who leaf through it identify with the bygone teens in the pictures? How relevant are age and era to the poems in here? As former hippy John Siddique's poem points out ('The same something', p.43):

> I am inside myself, all the ages of my life
> layering back to a point where there is just _____
> You might call it silence, but it is the fullest,
> brightest place, full of meaning, without words.

Siddique's wordlessness is one way to describe the fears and awkwardness of growing up, described later in Siddique's poem as that point 'when everyone else / answered NO, I wanted to say YES'. Norman MacCaig's persona in 'Ineducable Me' struggled to speak: 'I learned words, I learned words: but half of them / died for lack of exercise' (p.31). This anthology is an amusing, sometimes laugh-out-loud, witness to the differences between the personas we inhabit at sixteen and those we define as our selves at thirty and beyond.

Just as politicians need to be media-wise, *In Person: 30 Poets* (Bloodaxe, 2008) heralds an age advantageous to poets who can perform their work well while being filmed. In this fascinating anthology and DVD pairing, thirty poets appear on film reading their work, some catching the eye of the camera with a look of shyness or surprise. The films are very natural, appearing unrehearsed: many ask filmmaker Pamela Robertson-Pearce if it is all right to start, while some do practice runs of their introductions to camera. These behaviours are endearing, and perhaps their inclusion in the final film is designed to warm readers to the many brilliant poems, well-known and not so well-known, that proceed from anxious beginnings.

Robertson-Pearce filmed the poets in their living spaces in such diverse locations as Dublin, New York, Cardiff, Palestine, Spain, London, and Aldeburgh. Editor Neil Astley selected poets previously published by Bloodaxe, varied by gender (fourteen of the thirty poets are women, in keeping with an editorial policy of equal gender distribution). Nationality and heritage also vary with, for example, ten non-white poets. Menna Elfyn's lines in 'Welsh Ice' summon up the ad hoc nature of this anthologised community: 'We're scarcely a cobweb, a rumour of ghosts, / and a country might vanish at the turn of a key' (p.82). Twenty-eight of these poets were born before 1960, eleven before 1940. James Berry, born in 1924, is the oldest, and his reading, like many of the others, is both magisterial and sometimes halting. Thus this work serves as an archive as well as an anthology, with the merit of being accessible to anyone for a relatively small sum. It hardly matters whether, in the future, these poets are regarded as major or minor; as T.S. Eliot pointed out, an anthology should preserve both (p.1).

The criteria for inclusion suggest Astley's urge to educate readers about the poetic history of each of a broad set of poets. Anthologies have become more targeted at particular audiences, with carefully chosen sets of poets, since seventeenth-century printers randomly compiled poetic miscellanies from material lying around. While Astley has also used what he had to hand, *In Person* is overtly and proudly instructional, guiding readers in the value of pluralism. The poets appear in alphabetical order, and the cover image is a version, created by Astley and Robertson-Pearce, of a seventeenth-century painting by Pieter de Hooch: a white woman, perhaps illiterate, listens to her white husband reading a letter. On the wall hangs an 'old master' picture of Benjamin Zephaniah staring out from a wall of books, subverting the narrow frame of European literary culture. Indeed, *In Person* includes numerous political poems that salute change, perhaps as part of a poet's craft, as in John Agard's 'Bridge Builder' or Imtiaz Dharker's 'Honour Killing,' quoted in part here (p.59):

> Let's see
>> what I am out here,
>> making, crafting,
>> plotting
>> at my new geography.

This is the last stanza in a poem that queries the allegiances that bind us, 'a country / that I swore for years was mine' and 'a faith / that made me faithless / to myself.' Astley, creator of Bloodaxe, has appended a long essay on its history, explaining that his time working for *Stand* magazine made him aware of exiled or persecuted writers from Eastern Europe. Bloodaxe, he says, identifies as a left-wing press and supports poets who have written about political matters such as Zephaniah, Dharker and Jackie Kay, all included in this book. Giving a poet an opportunity to speak (as they are being filmed for the DVD that accompanies this book) alongside the page may help that poet's values be better understood. Perhaps that is why, as opposed to a themed collection, this anthology represents opportunities to identify a poem with its creator. It shows, though briefly, what sort of person wrote these lines.

References

Astley, N. and Robertson-Pearce, P. (eds) (2008) *In Person: 30 Poets*. Tarset: Bloodaxe Books.

Hannah, S., and Hegley, J. (eds) (2008) *The Ropes to Hold On To*. Newcastle upon Tyne: Diamond Twig.

Eliot, T.S. (1946) 'What Is Minor Poetry?', *The Sewanee Review*, 54 (1), pp.1-18. Available at: https://www.jstor.org/stable/27537650 (Accessed: 2 March 2024).

A Poet's Sense of Nonsense

Early in my poetry writing life, I invented a being called a thike. The thike broods, plays, and is 'othered' by an uncaring society. There are three poems about thikes in my second collection, *The Clockwork Gift*: 'The Thike', 'The Wild Life of Goodbye', and 'Sleeping on a Trampoline' (Shearsman, 2009). Over three poems, the thike develops: from an animal that is first cared for by its human community in 'The Thike', then attacked and destroyed as a species in 'The Wild Life of Goodbye' till, in the third poem 'Sleeping on a Trampoline', I describe a thike as a human being who is considered by their community as odd, alien and not fully human. I thought of the thike – I still do think of it – as a nonsense character. But why voice a thike at all if I think of these poems as nonsense?

We know what nonsense is: spoken or written words that make no sense or convey absurd ideas. Poetry is, of course, usually not as plain-spoken as prose; poetry can convey meaning through less than rational means. When you write a poem, it could be said that the clarity of your lines differs from that of prose, that in a poem there is a clarity of feeling or intuition rather than of meaning. Also, there is an ordered universe in a poem, but not always as you know order in daily life. Apart from the unusual, at times some would say nonsensical, structure found in poetry, there is a literary sub-genre of Nonsense, with identifiable features. Nonsense often employs certain poetic devices, such as lists of items that do not belong together (impossibilia), repetition, neologisms, assonance, and alliteration. But, you still might ask, why would a poet choose this poetic genre – why go so far from sense as to write Nonsense?

Perhaps, as in my case, the answer is partly because a poet will have loved Nonsense poetry as a child and continued to feel that attraction. Children love wordplay for its own sake; they are learning a language and are delighted to spot apparent mistakes, silly humour, and join in with sound-led repetition. I have never forgotten the illogical nursery rhymes and stories of my childhood, and I have been delighted to write Nonsense poems occasionally.

I acknowledge my invented creature, the thike, as nonsense, like other nonexistent beings such as the dong with the luminous nose (Edward Lear) or the snark (Lewis Carroll). In terms of Nonsense, though the actions are somewhat nonsensical, I don't use many nonsense words, and the settings are intelligible.

Why did I write the thike poems? We do most things for practical reasons, but in my case, I have never found a reason why I write any given poem. Who knows what drives a poem – could writing a poem be a nonsense activity in itself? I could say I write for readers, and some readers have apparently accepted the nonsense in these poems. Here's one comment by poet and critic David Wheatley, referring to the third thike poem in *The Clockwork Gift* (p.76):

> 'Sleeping on a Trampoline' ends with the richly absurd image of a thike so desperate to exit its mother's uterus it calls to a passer-by, threatening to jump. Like any good nonsense writing, Crowther's poem has no difficulty in making you 'agree to wrong / ideas'.

Of course, any poem can have nonexistent beings, symbolic or allegorical, but I invented a never-having-lived character. This is not the thike – I mean the narrator of each thike poem. The thike narrators are not me – they have met thikes whereas I never have. I know thikes don't exist and never have existed. I wanted to write about a never-having-existed character for my narrator to meet and tell readers about and, more than that, I wanted a never-can-have-existed character. I wanted readers to know the thike doesn't exist and can't have existed, at the same time as they are reading a coherent story about one – that is the nature of nonsense.

Nonsense, a breakdown of sense with a different sort of meaning, has a vast reach in poetry, where it ranges from the amusing to the terrifying. Arthur Rimbaud's poetry was ground-breaking in the late nineteenth century, and it has been written about as nonsense by critics. Rimbaud writes to Paul Demeny in 1871 (p.43):

> 'The poet makes himself a seer by a long, prodigious and rational disordering of all the senses. Every form of love, of suffering, of madness; he searches himself, he consumes *all* the poisons in him and keeps only their quintessences. …He reaches the unknown, and even if crazed he ends up by losing the understanding of his visions, at least he has seen them!'

How do you make sense of this? Poet and critic Archibald MacLeish wrote in an essay on Rimbaud's poetry (p.140):

> Poetry seems sometimes to regard itself not as an orderer of life but life's opposite and anti-end, and the deepest human need in certain generations has appeared to be a need not to make sense of our human lives but to make nonsense of them.

Certainly, MacLeish's personification of poetry speaks of the fissures in my own sense of reality. Maybe nonsense is one of the ways I experience my life as a human being. I try to express that experience in the thike poems, as if life is an encounter with a nonexistent being. Perhaps it is predictable that a poet like me would write Nonsense poetry; my first three collections have a style akin to what Stephanie Burt has called elliptical. In *Close Calls with Nonsense,* Burt wrote that elliptical poets have a voice that is 'hinting, punning, swerving away' from an obscure backstory, all traits of my own poetry (p.346). Poet and critic Richard Price noted, '[w]hile Crowther's poems may be crystal clear, more often they are riddling, varying, mysterious' (p.27).

I would suggest that, in addition to twelfth-century fatrasies, poems by Chaucer, Shakespeare, Edward Lear, Lewis Carroll, my thike poems, and countless other Nonsense poems through the centuries, all poetry is intimately connected with nonsense. According to Anna Barton, John Stuart Mill believed that, on first encountering a piece of writing, a reader might recognise its poetry before its meaning, and this 'does suggest that poetry stands at a certain remove from sense, that a poem might make nonsense before it makes sense' (p.313).

I wonder whether the process of reading a poem – getting that first hit of non-sense before sense dawns – is not so different from the process of writing a poem. You know you're writing a poem before you know what the poem might ultimately be saying. This is true for me – working through the early drafts of a poem can be a nonsensical process. That labour transforms the poem into something unexpected, whether the final draft is Nonsense or not. An early draft might be Nonsense, a later draft not. Edith Sitwell redrafted an early Nonsense poem into a decidedly not Nonsense, rational poem. She wrote that one of her early poems, 'Pompey', 'deliberately guttered down into nothingness meaninglessness', referring to these lines (p.xviii):

Said the Bishop,
Eating his ketchup:
'There still remains Eternity...'

This passage exhibits humour, rhyme, rhythm, and emotional detach-
ment, all characteristics of Nonsense poetry. Sitwell first wrote these lines
in what she called 'the moronic cackling of the 1920s' (p.xviii). Years later
she rewrote the same lines to convey the menace of war (p.xix):

Said the Bishop, 'The world is flat....'
But the see-saw Crowd sent the Emperor down
To the howling dust – and up went the Clown

In this version, the diocese has become a murderous crowd, and the
clown-like behaviour of the Bishop in the first version now results in
his death. We might think of Sitwell's process here as exemplifying what
Ludwig Wittgenstein said about nonsense, that it is a ladder you climb
up then throw away behind you. I like Wittgenstein's idea of the ladder
of nonsense. While I was writing *The Clockwork Gift*, I decided to use this
principle and make nonsense a tool in the generation of all of my poems.
While redrafting my poems, I would splice in an image, an idea, another
set of lines that would have nothing, as far as I could see, to do with the
existing poem. I would then spend months nuancing this hybrid into
coherence. The final poem might or might not be Nonsense.

Thus the emergence of nonsense in my poem does violence to the
original settled lines. Moreover, literal physical violence – battles, trials –
is a recurring feature of Nonsense poetry. Edward Lear's poem 'Mr and
Mrs Discobbolos' is an example. Here is one passage (p.325):

Mr. and Mrs. Discobbolos
        Climbed to the top of a wall
And they sat to watch the sunset sky
And to hear the Nupiter Piffkin cry
        And the Biscuit Buffalo call.
They took up a roll and some Camomile tea,
And both were as happy as happy could be –
        Till Mrs. Discobbolos said, –
        "Oh! W! X! Y! Z!

"It has just come into my head –
"Suppose we should happen to fall! ! ! ! !"

They don't fall, Mrs Discobbolos and the little Discobbolosses – instead Mr Discobbolos blows them all up!

Contemporary Nonsense poems also employ violence. Geraldine Clarkson's 'Spoiler', for example, describes a destructive nonsense character. Spoiler is a character who haunts houses while their owners sleep, looking for ways to spoil the good feelings with which they have gone to bed. In 'The Questionnaire', a Nonsense poem by Christian Morgenstern, the hero Korf loudly proclaims his non-existence to the Police Commissioner (p.157):

...the party signed below
does not actually occur

in conventional reality...

The authorities in this poem hound citizens, suggesting the nightmare of existence in a police state; Korf is being hounded and responds with a nightmare statement, that he does not exist. In 'The Wild Life of Goodbye', I wanted an intimation of military might to oppress my characters because, however nonexistent in real life thikes are, the poem is about the destruction of a species. I approached the military aspect gently, suggesting it in 'cruising panic run moon solder' (p.30). The words 'cruise', 'run', and 'solder' came into the poem during my nonsense process; I see them as suggestive of war.

Violence is only one recurring aspect of the Nonsense poem; there are other themes and devices, as many critics have enumerated. Numbers, for example, appear as an ordering device, and order is important, interestingly, in Nonsense poetry. The nonsense world is orderly, as critic Raymond Moody has said: 'Nonsense ... operates by its own coherent inner logic' (p.22). It is not an order that the reader can recognise from everyday life. Yet once unusual information has been introduced in a Nonsense poem (e.g. characters living on top of a wall), that will be taken seriously, and the poem's characters will behave as those living in such spaces would be expected to behave. In 'The Thike', the number five is important. There are ten stanzas, ten mentions of the word thike, and five uses of the letter k through the poem, in addition to its use in the five-letter word thike. The teacher in stanza five has published 90 books; there are 18 fives in 90, and the teacher exits the poem on line 18. Even though the reader is not necessarily aware of these qualities as they read, this use of numbers creates an inner logic to the poem.

Another aspect of Nonsense poetry is its use of repetition. Gertrude Stein's essay 'Composition as Explanation' suggests, as a tenet of poetics, that 'beginning again and again explaining composition and time is a natural thing' (Stewart, 1989, p.131). 'Sleeping on a Trampoline', my third thike poem, centres on rebounding, the game of continuously jumping on a trampoline (p.31):

> Usually a child takes my hand and up, whee,
> a few moments, then brings me down, my feet
>
> plunge into sturdy skin, the palm throws me
> back at a long day's sky like a duck, shuttlecock,
> bee, the smack of body against my bones,
>
> not-hug, not-massage, not-relax-you're-cared-for,
> only a continent moving by my right shoulder.

Rebounding exemplifies the never-getting-anywhere quality of much Nonsense poetry, because how can progress occur in the land of non-sensical action? Nonsense offers an endless game for the reader to play.

Another Nonsense poetry theme, class confusion, subverts social rules. Philip O'Connor in 'Poems' describes a world that operates differently to ours: 'gravely the assembled chimney stacks walked into the high street where the various wombs were displaying unborn children in Midnight Market' (p.150). In this prose poem, chimney stacks are living creatures, and wombs are fruit to be displayed in a market. In 'The Wild Life of Goodbye,' my second thike poem, I swapped human and non-human classes so that humans are feral and animals are humanised: a deer counts bank notes, a dog tugs at a child's paw. Taking the three poems as a sequence, the thike has become human by the third, final poem.

Confusion gives rise to a fourth aspect of Nonsense poetry, surprise. Nonsense poetry makes a virtue of surprise. Surprise, indeed, is part of all good poetry. In a lecture on surprise in poetry, Jane Hirshfield said, 'any creativity that matters must surprise' (p.48). A successful poem, in my view, evokes a world the reader has not previously encountered. Surprise has always played a role in Nonsense poetry. Within a conventional syntax and coherent logic, Nonsense poetry surprises and, usually, delights with its broken social rules, invented characters, sudden violence, and surreal twists in the narrative. There are countless examples of surprise in Nonsense poems. In the sixteenth century, John Taylor, famous as a Nonsense poet, wrote a long poem called 'The Essence … of Nonsense upon Sense' (Malcolm, 1997, p.27) in which he claimed to be a 'surprizer', a quality his Royalist audiences clearly valued, as they supported his readings in large numbers (Malcolm, p.22). Twentieth-century Nonsense poet Mervyn Peake offers many examples of surprise, often adding odd and striking details to his poems. In 'O'er Seas That Have No Beaches', he writes (p.37):

> I floated with twelve peaches,
> A sofa and a swan.

The juxtaposition is surprising: what have peaches to do with sofas and swans? This is a list of what was called, in classical and mediaeval literature, 'impossibilia'. Impossibilia was also known as adynaton, a poetic device that employs exaggeration to the point of impossibility. Such a list focuses on non-relationship among its parts so that the effort a reader makes to give the list unity provides not only surprise but intellectual effort. As the Queen advised Alice in *Alice Through the Looking Glass,* one needs to make an effort to believe impossible things; she herself practised believing six impossible things before breakfast (Carroll, 1897, p.102).

Building on the surprise of the thike's existence, I also included literary surprises in the thike poems. To confirm the thike's history, for example, I added past voices such as this supposed quote from a letter by Keats: '*I think upon crutches like the thikes / in your pump room*' (p.32). Readers have asked me whether Keats really wrote that. If you are open to the possibility that thikish beings have always lurked around the corner, you might also accept that a Romantic poet such as Keats would have been familiar with thikes. Keats's self-assessment, that he thinks upon crutches, is countered by the usually relaxed thikes. We learn that animal thikes 'fool near their wood' despite a high number of them being casually shot. A human thike quotes a nonsense children's rhyme in 'Sleeping on a Trampoline' (p.32):

It's not because I'm dirty
It's not because I'm clean
It's not because I kissed a thike
Inside a space machine

The thike could have quoted the serious-minded Keats or any other more rational lines, but she chooses Nonsense and bounces on the trampoline till dawn.

Apart from ordering, class confusion, violence, surprise, and impossibilia, there is another, subtler element that enhances a Nonsense poem: silence. Silence is a part of any poem, the space between stanzas, the space at the end of the line or within words on a line. Those silences lend themselves to Nonsense where the reader will find they pause their thinking at regular intervals, take a silent mental break, as the nonsense in the poem defeats their logic. In W.S. Graham's poem, 'The Beast in the Space', he describes a 'silence… on the other side of words'; there a 'great creature … thumps its tail … if you do not hear even that,' says the narrator, 'I'll give the beast a quick skelp / And through Art you'll hear it yelp' (p.157). Art uses the violence of form to make the silence speak; a 'skelp', for example, is a hard, violent touch and the word itself is made of a build-up, then sudden explosive release, of sound. It also sounds like 'help,' a cry from the victim of a skelping I have described the language non-human thikes use as touch, not understood by anyone else but the narrator of 'The Wild Life of Goodbye': 'I worked out how thikes talk by touch' (p.29). The animal thikes live in silence because, explains the narrator, 'thikes lack ears' (p.29) (physical aberration is another Nonsense poetry feature). Even the weather tends to silence in a pathetic fallacy that supports the tragic situation of the persecuted thikes: 'It was hot but I didn't notice how short of breath / the sky, how a summer lung can't speak / without breaking…' (p.29). The narrator separates sound and meaning when she explains that 'linguists charted [the thikes'] range of sounds; semantics no' (p.29). For a few seconds, as one first reads a poem, the brain hears only sound; then the meaning arises. Thus, sound comes before semantics in all poems including Nonsense poetry. Edith Sitwell, Dylan Thomas, and Louis Zukofsky, among many nonsense poets, have written sound-driven poems, occasionally leading to a rather abstract poem such as Sitwell's 'Portrait of a Barmaid' (p.166), not a purely Nonsense poem but tending that way:

Metallic waves of people jar
Through crackling green toward the bar,

[...]

Your soul, pure glucose edged with hints
Of tentative and half-soiled tints.

That last stanza edges towards Nonsense; the description of 'soul' as 'glucose' links to the later word 'glycerine', but how does 'glycerine' exude 'soul'? While the lines evoke striking visual and aural effects rather than a sense of reality, nevertheless this poem uses an everyday voice in its ways of speaking, as does most Nonsense poetry; there is no modernist fragmentation, no missing main verb, no unexpected grammatical construction. Usually, the surprise of a Nonsense poem arises from the strange narrative. In *Hellboy*, director Guillermo del Toro voices humans with satanically derived powers in a supposedly devilish manner, yet the character Hellboy, not human but a demon with scarlet skin, sawn-off horns and swishing tail, speaks as an Everyman would. This is no mistake: everyday language becomes odd alongside absurd behaviour. As Marjorie Perloff says about poetry composed of such everyday documents as police records, 'the more doggedly factual and informational the set of documents presented, the more it manifests a surreal edge' (p.167). The film viewer, like the reader of a Nonsense poem, expects normal behaviour from a character who speaks normally. When behaviour contrasts with speech, speech sparkles anew. The narrator of 'Sleeping on a Trampoline' relates the narrative anecdotally. She is designed to be believable, surprised at finding a mythical being in a supposedly idyllic contemporary village. She describes the village (p.32):

Some large houses, some small irregular roofs,
red, green, grey tiles, a pond to fulfil

the quality of life clause. Nobody said
there were still thikes.

Her later exclamations of 'oh!' and 'ooh!' voice the surprise inherent in the thike poems as in all Nonsense poems. The narrator of 'The Thike' says: 'The community is stunned. The prevalence / of a unique English animal / is like a local murder' (p.27). The narrator of 'The Wild Life of Goodbye' is similarly in a state of shock; she alone has cracked the language of a unique species that has now been destroyed. To show shock, her voice divides between lineated verse (alternating with prose poetry) and areas of silent space between stanzas.

One final element of some Nonsense poems is the use of such neologisms, such as the word 'thike'. Lewis Carroll was a superb creator of poetic neologisms, with such now-familiar words as 'mimsy' and 'borogove'. Dylan Thomas, in poems that I read as Nonsense, coined 'tigron' (p.110), 'manwaging' (p.42), and 'loudening' (p.49). I have written a love poem, 'UFood', in *On Narrowness*, composed almost entirely of neologisms (2015, p.60):

> You're goeshlivmicurmic.
> You're hoth, hith, huth, hith again.
> You're inmithed. You're always jecly or at least jey.
> You're krattles at the weekend. Kerp.
> You're lacemad fillets of freshwater.
> You're every munkid I ever cooked.
> You're nurma, you're nedbaked, you're nipwhisked.
> You're always ooove. Admit it, you're oan.
> You're not pixtunt yet (that's bitter).

These lines were a delight to invent and, because the entire poem is made of neologisms, I hope by line three or four to have trained the reader's ear to accept the device as essential to the poem.

There is one (not quite) neologism in the three thike poems: each narrator, confronted with a thike for the first time, says at least one word that will be unfamiliar to readers, the creature's name. While naming the thike gives a name to the non-existent, the word 'thike' is not a personal name; its use is dehumanising in the third poem, where the thike is a human being who is assessed by his neighbours as inferior and not fully human. A thike is a type of knife in Albania, and there is a river Thika in Kenya. But I made up my own meaning before checking its other denotations, as I wanted to invent a word for Nonsense reasons. As Gilles Deleuze explains, referring to the name Lewis Carroll gave the snark, you name a non-sense being so that it can say its own sense (pp.45-6). I arrived at the word thike via an anagram of my partner's name, Keith. Stewart says that the anagram is 'an example of the nonsense of arrangement and rearrangement within a closed field.'(p.176). Carroll, superlative Nonsense poet, loved anagrams, as evident in his creation of 'Flit on, cheering angel' from 'Florence Nightingale' (Abeles, 2005).

This word 'thike' is where I come closest to voicing a nonexistent being because I, not the narrators, named the thike. The word pre-exists the small world of the poem where the culture of the narrators, the landscape of fields, ponds and villagers, overlaps that of the individual poet. What I know, and the narrators can never know because they have met the thike, is that a thike is nonsense and does not exist. Anxious narrators who encounter thikes may provoke allegorising or symbolising observations in the reader, but the poet's underlying knowledge that there is no thike continually fractures such observations. I find it easier to examine where the truth, any truth, and the lack of it might reside. As Helena Nelson said, reviewing *The Clockwork Gift*, 'in the matter of obscurity...One is never in any doubt that something is going on and that all the poems are thinking about what that thing might be' (p.64). Nonsense makes light of obscurity: who has heard of a thike? The reader will discover something that they might suppose cannot exist and will be sure does not. Neither Nonsense poetry, the stuff of non-sense, nor any other poetry, offers a substitute for the hard reality with which we live. It unmakes reality so that we can, because we can deny it has meaning, look away from reality and, just briefly, relax.

REFERENCES

Abeles, F.F. (2005) 'Lewis Carroll's ciphers: The literary connections' in *Advances in Applied Mathematics* 34, pp.697–708.

Barton, A. (2009) 'Delirious Bulldogs and Nasty Crockery: Tennyson as Nonsense Poet', *Victorian Poetry* 47 (1), pp.313-330.

Burt, S. (2009) *Close Calls With Nonsense*. Minneapolis, MN: Graywolf Press.

Clarkson, G. (2023) *Medlars*. Bristol: Shearsman Books.

Crowther, C. (2009) *The Clockwork Gift*. Exeter: Shearsman Books.

Crowther, C. (2015) *On Narrowness*. Bristol: Shearsman Books.

Carroll, L. (1897) *Through the Looking Glass*. Philadelphia, PA: Henry Altemus.

Deleuze, G. (1990) *The Logic of Sense*. Translated by M. Lester and C. Stivale, edited by C.V. Boundas. London: The Athlone Press.

Snodgrass, W. D. (1998) *Selected Translations*. Rochester, NY: BOA Editions.

Graham, W.S. (2004) *New Collected Poems*. London: Faber and Faber.

Hirshfield, J. (2016) *Hiddenness, Uncertainties, Surprise: Three Generative Energies of Poetry.* Tarset: Bloodaxe Books.

Lear, E. (1943) *Nonsense Omnibus.* London: Frederick Warne & Co.

MacLeish, A. (1960) *Poetry and Experience.* London: Penguin Books.

Malcolm, N. (1997) *The Origins of English Nonsense.* London: Harper Collins.

Moody, R. (2020) *Making Sense of Nonsense.* Woodbury, MN: Llewellyn Publications.

Morgenstern, C. (1963) *Gallows Songs.* Translated by M. Knight. Berkeley, CA: University of California Press.

Nelson, H. (2007) 'More than meets the eyeballs', *Magma Poetry* 38, p.64-67.

O'Connor, P. (1987) *Surrealist Poetry in English.* London: Penguin Books.

Peake, M. (1974) *A Book of Nonsense.* London: Picador.

Perloff, M. (2010) *Unoriginal Genius: Poetry by Other Means in the New Century.* Chicago, IL: University of Chicago Press.

Price, R. (2009) 'Poetry in Brief', *Times Literary Supplement* 5559, p.27.

Rimbaud, A. (1995) Translated by O. Bernard in Rothenberg, J. and Joris, P. (eds). *Poems for the Millennium.* Berkeley, CA: University of California Press.

Sitwell, E. (2006) *Collected Poems.* London: Duckworth Overlook.

Stewart, S. (1989) *Nonsense: Aspects of Intertextuality in Folklore and Literature.* Baltimore, MD and London: The John Hopkins University Press.

Thomas, D. (1962) *Collected Poems 1934–1952.* London: J. M. Dent.

Wheatley, D. (2009) 'A striking talent', *New Welsh Review* 85, pp.75-76.

Wittgenstein L. (2001) *Tractatus Logico-Philosophicus.* London: Routledge Classics.

Preferring Poetry

Muriel Spark, *Complete Poems*
R.F. Langley *Complete Poems*

Had she written only *Complete Poems*, and knowing her novels as we do, it would be tempting to judge Muriel Spark a minor writer. She found writing novels far easier than writing poetry, but was suspicious of such facility. '[M]y outlook on life and my perceptions of events are those of a poet,' she claimed defensively in the Foreword to the 2004 edition of *Complete Poems* (p.xiv).

The poems in this collection hover between the departing surreal romanticism of 'forties poets such as Dylan Thomas and the coming social realism of Philip Larkin's Movement. A tone both of the surreal and the super-real, or perhaps the supernatural and wit, electrify her best poems. Here is the first stanza of 'Elementary' (p.54):

Night, the wet, the onyx-faced
Over the street was shining where
I saw an object all displaced
In black water and black air.

Here, the narrator separates, not from her soul or doppelganger or fetch, but from her body or rather from the shape of her body, which she has left behind as she moves along the street in the rain. She sees the vision as 'an object all displaced / in black water and black air' (p.54). The poem deals with Archimedes's principle of buoyancy in water, but also disclaims knowledge of science ('knowing little of natural law') and suggests, in the end, that her vision is closer to the supernatural than the physical: 'I can't describe what happens after / You weigh a body such as I saw / First in air and then in water.' (p.54).

Spark practised a variety of forms, including the sonnet, ballad, rondel, villanelle, and free verse. This variety gives a pace to the book that feels like restlessness, reflected in her frequent use of questions to structure poems, as in 'Is This the Place?' (p.89):

But really, is it the same place, that
Cosy old-fashioned bistrot we used to eat in

[...]

They've changed it completely, haven't they?
Or have they? This could be somewhere different.

The questions serve to analyse the nature of reality through time: does a memory, whether an individual or shared memory, guarantee the reality of the event remembered? The poem proceeds to decide that memory is wrong: 'It / Can't be the place' and could also be a portrait of a psychological waystation; other poems in this collection question various spiritual entities, such as angels, the dead, and those in Purgatory. Michael Schmidt, in his Afterword, refers to the 'spiritual battle' enacted in her longer poems (p.127). The narrator of 'Is This the Place?' likens it to a 'cosy old-fashioned bistrot', and 'yet / They've changed it completely, haven't they?' Much has changed but more has remained the same, as the poet eventually decides about the bistrot, resolving the question with a view of the proprietor, 'as old as ever... / Yes, this is the old place' (p.89). This poetic questioning of faith and spiritual reality works best when it appears brisk and aloof, a tone supported by end rhyme in 'Against the Transcendentalists' (p.55):

And so I reserve
The right not to try to
Fulfil the wilderness or fly to
Empyreal vacuity with an eye to
Publication, for what am I to
Byzantium or Byzantium
To me? I live in Kensington
And walk about, and work in Kensington

The question is rhetorical here, and further questions ('Who is Every-man...What is Truth true of?') present as existential nonsense (Spark is an excellent Nonsense poet). The result is: 'I therefore resign / The seven-league line / In footwear of super-cosmic design' (p.56). The final two lines suggest a Catholic resolution in her quest for the truth: 'Text is the thing defined, / The flesh made word' (p.56), if 'text' is the Bible and transubstantiation is what is meant by 'flesh made word'.

Perhaps the most significant poem in this collection is a surreal eighteen-pager. 'The Ballad of the Fanfarlo' resembles a horror film script set in a hospital (p.99):

Samuel Cramer laid his head down,
And he was locked in an anaesthetic sleep.
The ether-bowl stood over him
And the keen knife ripped him up.

And first they found his white bone,
And next his brown marrow,
And when they found his feverish heart
They said, 'He is No Man that we know...'

Steeped in symbolism, this poem draws on T.S. Eliot's 'The Waste Land' and Coleridge's 'The Ancient Mariner', as well as borrowing from Baudelaire's novella, *Fanfarlo*, in my view all examples of attempts to find spiritual truth within a mythic or surreal framework. Cramer is 'a man alarmed with fever' and emerges from his long, physically torturous battle for truth into a debate with Death (p.95). Death suggests Cramer is ready for a limbo of memory (known as Purgatory in Catholicism), but Cramer refuses to forget all that he has suffered. Death replies 'there's no scope for a talented type / In the loss of memory', as if the need to remember is a quality of the gifted, and the ordinary mortal may, thankfully, sleep through eternity (p.112). This poem and others in this collection reflect deeply on the role of memory and belief in life and death.

Apart from eight new poems of varying quality, this *Complete Poems* is the same as the *Complete Poems* published in 2004, with the ordering that Spark herself approved, not chronological but so lightly thematic that, on occasion, the thread reads simply like a word being echoed in adjacent poems. I would have preferred to see the poems chronologically arranged, to appreciate Sparks's development. But the personality in the poems never changes, and it breaks through the narrators she constructs to give us irresistible asides, such as this one in 'That Bad Cold': 'Nobody asked him to come. (Yes, / He is masculine, but otherwise / Don't try to parse the situation.)' (p.16). This turn to the audience by the narrator throws the poet's personification of a nasty cold as masculine into sudden relief and warns off any reader response; I find this warm and funny, even if disturbingly anti-men.

Until her first novel was published in 1957, Spark's adult life was devoted to poetry. She won prizes for her poems as a schoolgirl and served as editor of *Poetry Review* from 1947–1949, which put her at the centre of the British poetry establishment. But that job was no sinecure, and she eventually chose to be dismissed rather than resign. She achieved success as a novelist fairly rapidly and carried on writing poetry on the side. She never gave up her view of herself as a poet in spite of her greater reputation in prose.

R.F. Langley (1938–2011) is a poet of observation of the natural world, and *Complete Poems* unites all he can salvage of his many insights. Nature is only one element. Other rich material pre-exists in the poet's mind and glitters in the wordscape, hence editor Jeremy Noel-Tod's inspired inclusion of short bibliographies to indicate what Langley was reading during a poem's gestation. 'Achilles', for example, starts with painterliness (p.128):

> One is seldom directed by way of
> an indigo gate. A life is plunged in
> colours, saturations, shades, tints, hues. One
> screws one's eyes up.

Then Langley throws into the mix Achilles's murder of Penthesileia, seventeenth-century gentlewoman Elizabeth Havers, the rock-breaking power of a tree, Newton and his prism, and ends with a wading heron. Langley's particular and original observations depict the closeness of humans to animals, birds and inorganic matter. In 'My Moth: My Song', nature (the moth) meets the poet (p.103):

> It goes on. Hawk moths stammer in front of
> the red valerian. These words, floated
> in the silence, by myself, hover close
> to my thoughts. The thoughts themselves almost were
> words. I think they were. I think they did. How
> close is close? What colour were the moths?

The moths have become words or, like people, Langley describes the moths as stammering. Langley is so imbued with the nature he observes, thinking about it, writing about it, and of course being in it, that his sense of reality and the real boundaries between humans and nature, slip: 'The thoughts themselves almost were / words. I think they were. I think they did.' (p.103). His enjambment here suggests a shifting of realities, word to moth, thought to word, non-existent to existent: a poem demands that a word should have as much physical reality as a moth.

Writing nature through words, which may include quotes from other texts, referencing other poets' descriptions, must have been encouraged by Langley's day job as an English teacher. Langley's teacherliness, developed over a lifetime in secondary schools (he became Head of English at Bishop Vesey grammar school in Sutton Coldfield and stayed there till retirement to Suffolk in 1999), shows in countless mentions of classroom commonplaces, such as raising hands, being late, ticking answers. His studiousness, the art of paying attention to his surroundings, is exemplary in his great later poems, though some early and brilliant poems, such as 'The Ecstasy Inventories', show signs of the discipline needed to express moments in time with all their physical and mental activity (p.16):

> Take now and make a then.
> A room. A roomy workshop. Elderflowers.
> Forget the scent. Here is a carpenter,
> singing. It is a hymn. Never mind
> the scent, forget the difficult
> bushes.

This is a picture of poet as builder, jettisoning main verbs, making one part of speech do the work of another, using punctuation to cement together parts of lines and sentences. Langley could skim the plaster perfectly, as in 'Juan Fernandez': 'But command is taken now by those tiny / expert birds who perch, and glow, and whizz / and pick the pepper out of the closing air. (p.24). These lines smooth all grammatical awkwardnesses; the sound pattern of the consonants in 'expert birds who perch', and wit, in 'pick the pepper out of the closing air', are not strained but accurate and even relaxed.

Many such gorgeous sound patterns, echoing Gerard Manley Hopkins, form typically long stanzas with assonance and alliteration, as evident in the last poem, 'To a Nightingale', posthumously awarded the Forward Prize for Best Single Poem. It creates a retiring narrator ('No business of mine') at the same time as the narrator openly admits his presence (p.153):

No business of mine. Mites which
ramble. Caterpillars which
curl up as question marks. Then
one note, five times, louder each
time, followed, after a fraught
pause, by a soft cuckle of
wet pebbles, which I could call
a glottal rattle. I am
empty, stopped at nothing…

'A soft cuckle of / wet pebbles, which I could call' suggests to me that the poet's voice could do what the nightingale does and thus could deliver a nightingale's song. Langley indicates this by his line break, 'which I could call', and the sentence then, having established the connection of poet and song, carries on to finish the description of the birdsong as 'a glottal rattle': poets and their songs bestride the globe just as nightingales migrate from the UK to Africa in winter. Song is the business of the nightingale as well as the poet, more than, say, rambling and curling up by the fireside in winter.

This is not a collection to read once and put aside. From time to time, choose a page or two, and study them as you would a meditation on the closeness of humans and nature.

REFERENCES

Langley, R.F. (2015) *Complete Poems*. Manchester: Carcanet Press.
Spark, M. (2015) *Complete Poems*. Manchester: Carcanet Press.

Telling the Truth

John Peck, *Cantilena*

The epigraph to John Peck's poem *Cantilena* (Shearsman, 2016), is a quote from Kafka's story of capital punishment, 'From the Penal Colony'. It describes a machine whose glass teeth take twelve hours to inscribe the words of judgement bloodily and fatally onto the body of the condemned, yet the process is exalted as enlightening by the narrator. *Cantilena* addresses such a problematic execution, not least through a somewhat arduous literary experience: the poem is 324 pages long, each page is a canto with densely blocked text, and there is unremitting intellectual rigour. If you finish it, your exhaustion might be rewarded with a sort of masochistic joy.

Who is John Peck? Though supported by British publishers (Carcanet, Shearsman), few in Britain seem aware of his work. He was born in Pittsburgh, Pennsylvania, wrote a PhD thesis on Ezra Pound, has written ten previous collections, has taught at university, and has also practised as a Jungian analyst. As *Cantilena* demonstrates, his poetry is intellectual and politically informed as well as literary. He has described how these interests interact: 'a focus upon viable politics often draws us into just that sudden deepening of intuition, that vertical sense of above and below, which tangles us in the life of dreams, psyche, and the disenfranchised terminologies of spirit' (1981, p.209). This passage suggests the breadth of both the psychological and intellectual challenges presented by Peck's work. In conversation with poet and critic John Matthias (p.179), Peck gives these challenges a spiritual context:

'Such scope is impersonal, although [...] it also embraces an examination of conscience. Impersonal, in that gravity has long been at work on metaphysics, condensing a steady rain of falling bodies from the heaven of ideas into the human psyche.'

Reading *Cantilena,* a lengthy poem rife with ideas and historical detail, offers an exciting sense of a curation of the museum of one's mind.

There is a long English poem by George Ripley (1415–1490), on which Freud gave a commentary, also called *Cantilena*. It is said to be the first English poem on alchemy. Canto 50 of the third section (called a span) of Peck's *Cantilena* blends war and science to show what gold can be transmuted from, for example, mixing belief in *salvator mundi* with research into atoms (p.202):

> The point was to win –
> grabbing after a fire that seared retinas
> swart with effulgence, a sinterizing same
> against same, opposition
> all the keener for that – a fathering masher
> launching the stretch limo of mortality
> into zero gravity, orgasmic worm splendor.
> A rumble sustained inside attraction itself
> hard against the boundary, alchemists
> calculating a discus throw from the salvator mundi
> to a savior working the power reaches of atoms,
> bronze plowing earth, Adam's grunting exhale into
> reunion. John Paul Vann
> barreled his pistol jeep down Vietnam's back roads
> believing he could map the void zones
> in his bosses' outlook, Emerson wired
> the circuit breakers past overload, cartography
> and mystic welds their double-column bookkeeping
> for enlarging a shared darkness
> through jumped-up light.

The canto is filmic and expresses the horror of Kafka's epigraph. Many of the descriptive phrases – 'orgasmic worm', 'void zones', 'shared darkness' – are reminiscent of horror tropes. With all the violence that the book contains, nevertheless, this extensive poem is a lyric, not a narrative: 'cantilena' as 'the melody or air in any composition' and 'an old song, silly prattle' (*Oxford English Dictionary*, 2005, p.847). From Italian, *cantilena* translates simply as 'song'. Yet Peck gives his lyric epic proportions; he is a conductor of long sweeps of lines, each canto unbroken by multiple stanzas. Musicality makes the intellectual content more vivid, and perhaps Peck's plaiting of accentual and syllabic lines with free verse strengthens the reader's 'mental ear', in J.H. Prynne's phrase, to manage the flow of ideas: 'Thus this poem lays out spans at 6s & 7s with themselves / because I count cadence / to push past my own glottal stoppage— ' (p.143).

This quotation typifies the ease with which Peck addresses the reader, explaining devices intended to assist in reading 350 pages of a single poem. Throughout this verbal forest, melodious phrases as well as syntactical surprises lighten the general density. Here is the first section of canto 68, section four (p.294):

> The immense releasing courage of caring hands,
> two-way pulses on through,
> something returns, but nothing wills that, palms outward,
> thus in the ikon the lost horses
> of stonemason martyrs Florus and Laurus
> return to the pond
> their dead owners gentling them, they gulping
> from a second sky lips curled, arcs widening and crossing
> through cloud resuming its blinding face
> on the calm there.

This is a ten-line sentence with many dependent clauses. Some adjectives are consoling, such as 'releasing' and 'caring,' while others are frightening: 'immense', 'lost', 'dead', 'blinding'. The participles 'gentling', 'gulping', and 'widening' suggest an ongoing flow, which is the dominant feel of this mighty river of a poem.

Canto 85a, section four, ponders the poetics of music and exemplifies the self-reflective capacity of a long poem (p.312):

> [*The sound is fading away, it is of five sounds, freedom*
> *the sound is fading away, it is of five sounds*
> and what this Ojibway song accomplishes
> *is beyond analysis* (Winters). Thus
> the mind in it eludes us, or waits on ahead.
> Three sounds reach me, they are of crossings:
> one sound is flowing away, it curls window-high, Florence
> in flood, a gondola on patrol.
> One sound shushes and melts, it is of two, four, eight sounds,
> panthers in tidal sands, the pre-dawn.
> One sound is coming apart, it is forty sounds, black freedom,
> a tinkling shower, shattered skylight littering
> see-through runes: Odin pats his flipped coat collar, satisfied
> that the night over Svalbard will see

not Walton pushing his men across ice, but trooped hazes.
That the expeditionary bones, pitted like Gravneset Glacier,
will teem with the horde's heat.
That my tinkling defenestration will grant me fresh air
by decapitating my Alpha
and threading on past Zed, in inky cold prior to defilements
and following the hunt. *Storm light, all unsent for.*
For images are to be flayed,
their meat eaten, their skins cured and worn,
even zeroed and oned and made current.]

The almost prosy start to this passage, 'what this Ojibway song accomplishes', moves on through a bracketed passage that feels like a diversion from the whole canto, describing how poetic meaning can be hard to reach as 'the mind in it eludes us', but that the sound of the song (the poem here) delivers meaning. Then the passage exemplifies and, simultaneously, describes that idea, as in 'One sound shushes and melts, it is of two, four, eight sounds, / panthers in tidal sands, the pre-dawn'. 'Two, four, eight' suggests the pace of a panther's padding feet as it hints at a child's game of chase: 'two four six eight, I'm coming to get you'. The final three lines are a description of Peck's poetry: 'images are to be flayed', not left unexplored. The poet is like Walton, a fictional (in Mary Shelley's *Frankenstein*) expeditionary leader into areas they can't survive and should not spoil.

Peck certainly wrings dry his images through more than one canto and his words, too. His word for section, 'span', is an example. Each section is a span in the sense of a bridge between parts, extending over, or spanning, time, within and beyond the twentieth century. 'Span' also has a narrative dimension, as in 'lifespan'. Here is one canto (canto 66, span one) of many in *Cantilena*'s roll-call of heroes (p.80):

Helen Nearing took her violin to Europe,
Krishnamurti proposed to her on the boat back,
but she went for Scott the Professor, who went after our life-ways
with masonry hammer. Fired out of his chair,
he built their stone house beneath Stratton, lecturing
cross-country to workers, not cowering then,
in age raising stone rooms two states closer to sunrise.
What have we not heard and ignored?

The blue poops of the galleons bobbed at Lisbon
behind the useless breakwater, the auroras
of a shaken winter unroll their snap and flash.
Nearing hauls water in a steel pail.
The structure of aluminum rays out
into the bauxite and copper steals in East Timor,
the slaughter lists for Jakarta sear in the siroccos of Iraq
laced with dust uranium, children's cancer wards
stripped of meds *usable as weapons,*
nor would Nearing have stepped clear of this giddy winefat,
shirt and overhauls stained with his own red.
Scrolls of the Northern Lights ripple at the pail's brim,
now haematose, now key lime,
sloshing the pole of inaccessibility
lodged in plain sight. I would rather not
have seen any of it, but I cannot forget.

There is a nursery lilt to the first three lines. Helen Nearing (1904-1995) was a formidable woman whose husband is introduced in line three along with his life's work of raising awareness of important social issues, such as colonial exploitation of precious minerals and the health risks to local children from mining uranium. That political activism, though aimed at peace, becomes violent imagery in *Cantilena*. Indeed, *Cantilena* presents a disquisition on violence, as its epigraph from Kafka suggests. To show the experience being communicated, Peck has Scott 'fired out of his chair' in line four, a phrase cleverly enjambed to hold back the literal meaning just for a second. Line five allows biography a more sedate rhythm: 'He built their stone house beneath Stratton, lecturing / cross-country to workers…', but the Nearings' hauling water in a pail, in line twelve, suggests poverty and consequent physical suffering. There are two reflective sentences among the storylines in this canto. The first carries the book-long enquiry: 'What have we not heard and ignored?' That question is addressed by the last two lines: 'I would rather not / have seen any of it, but I cannot forget.' Peck's thorough examination of the Nearings family and supporters, formed of *Cantilena*'s many independent-minded naysayers, push the poem to moral conclusions. There is vignette after vignette of those who have lived and died for others, for free speech, against fascism. But there is no 'them and us' in Peck's poetry. 'We share a self with others', he writes, and those others include, at the very least, our dead forebears. Peck's personal narrative focuses on his father, Clarence Peck, who was an engineer (p.74):

> Through old pasture road to a siding for tilt hoppers,
> at four peering from pillows in the front seat,
> with Father the furnace wizard pointing as slag ruptures
> to orange, cinnabar, shiny black.
> Such are the antipodes of my pastorals:
> untended meadows soon to be parceled,
> and disheveled powers seeking repose, as if
> setting building stones next to the dead sans inscriptions.

Clarence appears as magus and alchemist. In the following lines, Paul Dirac, a scientist who refused to join the Manhattan Project, is paired in passing with Clarence (p.95):

> Dirac thought he might separate U-235
> from heavier U-238 either by spinning them
> or varying temperature however
> slightly across the chamber. That last bit overlaps
> with my Father's process engineering
> for a long second then dissolves...

Putting Dirac's idea of 'varying temperature' alongside his father's engineering practice cannot elucidate all the work of either but conveys a vivid portrayal of their practice. Perhaps this is an example of what Peck called 'incarnational' truth: 'neither ideal nor an idea but incarnate' as he said in an interview with Clive Wilmer, meaning, I think, that ideals and ideas can be embodied, in actions that can be depicted, as here in *Cantilena* (Wilmer, 1994).

If you have gathered that Peck is hard work to read, given the density of allusion in the book and the sheer length at nearly 400 pages, that's not wholly true. It is not a radical read, technically speaking. Seemingly discursive, lateral, and full of asides, in fact this is a maze and a place to get lost. Nor is *Cantilena* just a breathtakingly long run of cantos. It's organised, in four sections, each engaging with such topics as politics, art, and climate change, to name just a few. Peck's references are so extensive that, were he to include notes within the text (as does that other North American elder of political poetry, admired by Peck,

Peter Dale Scott), each page would contain more footnotes than lines of poetry. Peck includes himself in the text from line one ('My paper-covered half pillar / near the door to hold letters...') and presents himself, in the light of the epigraph from Kafka's machinery of torture, as both scourger and scourged (p.143):

> Thus in obligation to the separated,
> impossibly I would narrate the undeniable
> in what they might have denied to the end, inscrutable
> in some part even to themselves,
> as Hoffman suffered the hurt
> of both not hearing
> and nearly going unheard. Saving hurt!

Peck admits, while *Cantilena* gives a witness to our problematic species, his task – to tell a story that is true but has been denied by its protagonists 'to the end' – is 'impossible' (p.143). Civic responsibility starts with this long, thorough and painful narration of 'the undeniable'.

REFERENCES

Peck, J. (1981) 'Our Politics and "The Dream of Private Clitus"', *Ploughshares*, 6 (4), pp. 208-227. Available at: https://www.jstor.org/stable/40348625 (Accessed: 3 March 2024).

Peck, J. (2016) *Cantilena: One Book in Four Spans*. Bristol: Shearsman Books.

Matthias, J. (2014) 'At Large: A Selection from *Cedars of Liban* in John Peck's *Cantilena*', *Notre Dame Review*, 39, pp.178-185.

Wilmer, C. (1994) 'John Peck in Conversation', *PN Review*, 98, 20 (6). Available at:https://www.pnreview.co.uk/cgi-bin/scribe?item_id=10243;hilite=Clive%20Wilmer (Accessed: 4 March 2024).

Confessing to Syllabics

'I too, dislike it', Marianne Moore said, referring to poetry, and she must have included syllabic poetry because she was and remains its pre-eminent practitioner in English (p.27). This opinion is not uncommon. Contemporary syllabics, where the organisational principle in the line is the number of syllables, never was and still isn't popular. Peter Groves has listed the judgments of Basil Bunting ('silly'), Michael Hamburger ('cannot see the point'), Adrian Henri ('redundant'), Peter Levi ('uninteresting'), and John Heath-Stubbs ('totally spurious') (p.123). Thom Gunn, discounting his own superb examples, said he used syllabics only to move from traditional English metre to free verse (p.xxxi). Donald Hall, like Gunn, also credits syllabics as a waystation in his poetic process: 'Syllabics was a way of holding on to number while avoiding iambic. I rhymed on the off-stress, pretending that English was French. From syllabics I took the leap to various types of free verse. I felt this necessity to break out of this cage I had made for myself' (Hall and Lammon, 1993, online). But even Gunn's and Hall's use of syllabics doesn't seem to have improved its reputation. I know poets who write in syllabics, but hate to be asked about it and dismiss the fact.

I am fascinated by the syllable in poetic activities. The syllable is the conventional, language-led atom in every English-language poem. Like an atom, it isn't the smallest part of material, typically consisting of a consonant plus a vowel plus perhaps another consonant, but it's wonderfully elastic. It can be as simple as *O* and as complex as *Christ*. Counting a syllable as one unit can't confine a line any more than counting a foot in an iambic pentameter will straitjacket a poet's rhythmic variety.

My fascination isn't original. Creating a poetic line by counting the number of its syllables has been practised in too many languages to list. The English syllable has been under discussion for centuries. Languages have different ways of using what we call syllables, varying their weight, duration, stress, and accent. Robert Bridges, British poet laureate from 1915 to 1930, a period when poets and critics argued about the syllable's contribution to metre, took syllables seriously. Influenced by Milton, he tried using syllabic effects derived from Latin in his major and most popular work, *The Testament of Beauty*. It's numbingly hard to read nowadays (though I find the loss of final Es for short-syllable words like 'hav' appealing). The syllable count for each line is twelve; that depends, in some lines, on eliding syllables, not always an easy process. For example, consider the passage: 'where plunging down the rocks they swam in the salt sea / to drowning death; nor hav they in acting thus today / any plan for their journey or prospect in the event' (p.23). The first line is easily counted and has the normal twelve syllables. The second line has thirteen syllables and can be reduced to twelve by eliding the central part of 'nor have' into one syllable 'nor've'. The third line counts as fourteen but can be reduced to twelve by eliding 'journey or' to 'journey'r' and 'the event' to 'th'event'. Many such elisions sound unnatural to a contemporary reader and raise the question of the necessity of sticking rigidly to a line syllable count when other forms of lineation do not keep to their established form; iambic pentameters, for example, frequently substitute their iambs for trochees or spondees.

Bridges's efforts at creating a modern long syllabic poem had a welcome result: it influenced his daughter, Elizabeth Daryush, who understood from her father that the normal speech stresses of English syllables could offer an exciting approach to measure differing from traditional metric verse. She also realised that a breakdown in a major form of poetic regulation, the traditional use of metre, could enable her poems to convey a post-First World War society, which she saw as disrupted if not broken (Davies, pp.43-51). Daryush was not the only poet to define poetry, metre and syllable in a social context. Writing from a postcolonial perspective, Zulfikhar Ghose supported modern English syllabics during a spat in the *Times Literary Supplement* in the 1960s; he saw such formal control as reining in the language of empire while throwing off imperialism (p.53). Daryush is possibly the first English poet to write in modern syllabics, as I defined it above, where the simple counting of syllables in a line forms the organisational principle. In 1934, she included a note in *Verses: Fourth Book* (adding it also as an appendix to her *Selected Poems* in 1972), a collection mixing metrical with syllabic poems (1972, p.93):

The poems without line-capitals are those written in syllabic me-tres (by which I mean metres governed only by the number of syllables to the line, and in which the number and position of the stresses may be varied at will) and are so printed as a remind-er to the reader to follow strictly the natural speech-rhythm, and not to look for stresses where none are intended.

This statement defines English-language syllabics for the next hundred years at least. The phrase 'natural speech-rhythm' marks an important part of the syllabic effect for Daryush and her followers. She wanted to release her poems from the iambic-led poetry that, through previous centuries, had made the word 'poetic' instantly identifiable as a rhythm. Her most famous poem, perhaps, is 'Still-Life' (p.30):

> Through the open French window the warm sun
> lights up the polished breakfast table, laid
> [...]
> rolls in a napkin, fairy rack of toast...

Conversational speech rhythm resists the ghost of metre in these lines: while the opening line similarly resists consistent metrical patterning, 'rolls in a napkin, fairy rack of toast' is a trochee-led but a mainly iambic line. Matthew Francis, one of the most able contemporary British syllabicists, echoed Daryush's reasoning in a private letter to me: 'Avoiding metre is part of the point, because [syllabics] allows a far greater rhythmic variety than is possible in metrical verse; I found my [syllabic] lines sounded more natural and conversational' (2015). Daryush's stanza above is more natural and conversational than previous poetry she had written. Here is a stanza from another early morning poem published by Daryush: 'I saw fair Fortune, one clear morning, touch / Like the bright-sceptred sun's first point of scorn, / With slightest finger my full-ripen'd corn' (1921, p.32). These mainly iambic pentameters are redolent of an era that believed in its right to rule ('fair Fortune', 'bright-sceptred') while suggesting problems are coming ('first point of scorn'). Dayrush's later poem about morning, quoted earlier, also has a whole stanza as a single sentence, but she has made notable changes: capitals at the beginnings of lines are removed, decreasing the emphasis on their first words. Daryush gives a sense of the quotidian with her details: breakfast table and toast rack rather than Fortune's fair finger at dawn, the sensuous poetic so notable in her non-syllabic poems. Yet the less conversational end rhymes and subtly patterned alliterations and assonances in 'Still-Life' remain despite the syllabics. The syllabics that Bridges, Daryush's father, used – the Latinate weighting of syllables – is different to the syllabics English-language poets use today. Octavio Paz, for example, saw accentual poetry, such as the poetry of Coleridge, as rebelling against syllabically controlled metres; pre-twentieth-century theorists had differentiated between the two (p.61). W.H. Auden wrote a clerihew, amusingly examined by Dave Collard, who points out that '"Bysshe" was pronounced with two syllables in Auden's day' whereas now it would be pronounced with one and thus render this clerihew imperfect (Collard, 2013):

> Among the prosodists, Bysshe
> Was the syllable-counting old sissy
> Guest
> The accentual pest.

Auden himself became very interested in syllabic poetry, first through reading Bridges's experiments in 1929 and, later, Marianne Moore. He was much influenced by Moore's syllabics: 'in 1935, [Auden] discovered Marianne Moore's thoroughly modern syllabics… [and] transformed syllabic verse into one of the great permanent resources of English poetry' (Mendelson, p.86). Auden's clerihew could have been written about prosodists writing far earlier than Edward Bysshe in *The Art of Poetry* (1702) and Victorian Edwin Guest. Sir Philip Sidney wrote in *Apology for Poetry* in 1583: 'Now, of versifying, there are two sorts, the one ancient, the other modern; the ancient marked the quantity of each syllable and according to that framed his verse; the modern observing only number (with some regard of the accent)' (Needham, p.60). Sidney didn't mean by the modern what Daryush meant by syllabic poetry; he meant that accentual-syllabic poems count both syllables and beats. One of the wonders accentual-syllabic poets can perform is to train the ear so that, while in everyday speech you might not actually pronounce a phrase in such a way that it fits a metrical pattern, in the poem that phrase is pronounced both ways at the same time. For example, James Fenton's poem 'The Ballad of the Shrieking Man' uses a four-beat line with eight syllables (Shapcott and Sweeney, p.130). The regularity of the beat in this poem about dancing is strong throughout. Halfway through the poem, an 'old codger' is 'forced… out to join the dance'. The dancing rhythm results in a stress on the second, fourth, sixth and eighth syllables; yet if you were saying this sentence aloud, you would naturally put the stress of the first half of the line more equally on the second and third words, or perhaps even on the second, third and fourth words. Having had many verses already to set up the rhythm unmistakably in my mind, I hear it both ways.

By Coleridge's time, accentual poems counted only beats, and modern syllabic poems counted only syllables. This means both syllabic and free verse poets must rely on the speech stresses of everyday diction; their poems don't set up a metrical pattern that can override normal speech patterns.

Syllabics offers its own benefits. For one, syllabics can work closely with the page. Cheap paper and the digital document have encouraged an exploitation of the space around words. In her zeal to represent contemporary speech, Daryush, in her abandoning of line capitals, shows that syllabics encouraged her to develop her typography. Her father also developed his; *The Testament of Beauty* does not use line-capitals, while his accentual lyrics do. Line capitals' unnatural stress remained popular for half a century more. Other poets, such as Moore and Dylan Thomas, used syllabics to dominate the page visually. They allow their syllabics to create significant and striking single or repeating shapes on the page, such as a cross. B.S. Johnson wrote a 'Note on Metre' as an afterword to his 1964 poetry collection and made this point: 'Since most poetry reaches its audience in printed form, a metre which is easily apprehended visually, as any syllabic one is, would seem to be more appropriate than those metres which depend upon sound, like stress or quantitative ones' (p.53). Matthew Francis demonstrates in 'Ocean' (p.18):

> The surface of the ocean. It's too deep here for waves.
> [...]
> you're closer to it than you might be
> [...]
> the deep blue world.

Francis creates a shape for this poem that suggests both depth and surface. His choice of a repeating stanza of declining syllabic lines is well suited to the swell of ocean waves.

Rather than make their own, many poets choose an existing stanza shape for their syllabic poem. The cinquain is a much-loved syllabic form invented by Adelaide Crapsey, and it seems to rustle the paper it's written on in her 'Night Winds' (p.32). This syllabic pattern is 2 / 4 / 6 / 8 / 2, and the poem is scenically rich. Interestingly, 'Night Winds' allows two meanings to emerge from the final line, 'Should weep', governed by reading a stress on the first or second word: Is the poet being told to weep? Or told something that makes her weep? There is an iambic lilt throughout the poem, suggesting the latter. At the same time, the syllabic pattern, picking out the contested phrase in two single-syllable words, helps resist the lilt, which is a strength here, in my view, a doubling effect in a poem wholly governed by a question.

A long poem composed of cinquain stanzas, such as Rachel Wetzsteon's 'Commands for the End of Summer', gives a sense of the 2 / 4 / 6 / 8 / 2 syllabic rhythm as much as accentual metre could. What if Wetzsteon had varied one of the stanzas to be, instead, 2 / 4 / 4 / 8 / 2? Should not the pattern be consistent? However, a poem's lines in iambic pentameter may be strictly iambic for, say, as little as twenty-five per cent of the time. Monotony is fatal to a successful poem. So why shouldn't the syllabic line vary occasionally from its set pattern? Can't the reader learn the regular repeat of a syllabic line? Therefore, won't the reader trust the poet to deliver the number of syllables promised? And if they find the number differs, if they feel duped, why should they? The reader might disapprove of variation even when the poem is successful as a whole. Many excellent syllabic poems offer occasional miscounted lines. Matthew Francis points out that 'both Daryush and W.D. Snodgrass miscount the syllables in places, and the fact that this doesn't make any real difference to the effect of the poem is an interesting theoretical problem' (2015).

Perhaps the major source of disagreement between fans of syllabics and naysayers is a question that has not been, and possibly cannot satisfactorily be, answered: how do you define or categorise contemporary syllabics? Is it, helpfully, a metre? Some say yes because metre means counting, and a syllabic poet counts syllables. B.S. Johnson defended what *The Spectator* had referred to in 1962 as a 'new fad' (p.53):

> Defining metre as the meaningful arrangement in regular patterns of one (or, rarely, more) of the constituent elements of language, it is as legitimate to use syllables as the elements from which to form metrical units as it is to use elements like stress or quantity.

Yet many believe a syllabic form is not truly measured because they do not hear the count of syllables. In that case, some argue, the syllabic poem is actually free verse. At least there is more measure in a syllabic line than in prose. In fact, if you use a regular five-syllable line, you will hear a two-beat metre in the background, as many on both sides of the argument have pointed out. The ten-syllable line offers the choice of an occasional strict pentameter, and it's easy to include lines with odd numbers of syllables when you want to vary the rhythm.

The rhythm of syllabics is discounted by many critics. Poet-critic Timothy Steele says there being no pattern of accent is a principle of syllabic verse. Steele's point is an important one. Just when a regular iambic or trochaic line starts to be discernible in a syllabic poem, it is thrown off course by a line without a regular rhythm. Some poets in the prehistory of modern syllabics have employed this device, as in these lines by John Donne in 'Satyre V' (p.149):

> Then man is a world; in which, Officers
> Are the vast ravishing seas; and Suiters,
> Springs; now full, now shallow, now drye; which, to
> That which drowns them, run. These self reasons do
> Prove the world a man, in which, officers
> Are the devouring stomacke, and Suiters
> The excrements, which they voyd. All men are dust

The breakdown of an iambic metre adds meaning to Donne's critique of courtly life by subverting the pentameter so completely that he was accused of only counting syllables. When I read the lines 'Springs; now full, now shallow, now drye; which, to / that which drowns them, run. These self reasons do / prove the world a man...', I find I read them as prose, not as any kind of metre, iambic or otherwise. As ten-syllable lines they make the point of the stanza very well: the court is corrupt; those who want to be there,the 'excrements', are disgusting. A steady rhythm would not convey this sentiment effectively nor would a regular rise and fall of syllables. The court, the poem, and each line, are a mess.

A contrast between the sound and the appearance on the page can create a pleasing dissonance, as Moore also knew. Her famously complex stanza patterns of syllabic lines contrast effectively with conversationally long sentences, as in the last two stanzas of 'The Fish' (p.39):

> ac-
> cident – lack
>   of cornice, dynamite grooves, burns,
>   and
>   hatchet strokes, these things stand
>   out on it; the chasm-side is

dead.
Repeated
  evidence has proved that it can
   live
    on what can not revive
   its youth. The sea grows old in it.

There's pressure to read the sentence simply as one long flow and ignore the line breaks. But the breaks are visually present, and I stop briefly at each one. After two or three stanzas, I feel as if I can hear the poem's shape. Moore struggled with her syllabic patterning, as evidenced by her dramatic revisions of poems throughout her life. The pattern of 'The Fish' changed from the early version above and lost the single syllable lines – 'this,' 'and,' 'live' – so that those single words appear on the lines preceding them. The later version is slightly less stilted than the original, but I feel that reading is a similar experience in both versions.

Moore also used syllabics to create lines from material found in scientific prose, as does contemporary English poet David Morley. He explains his process:

> I have broken some scientific prose verbatim into counted syllabic lines; I have placed episodes of linked description into stanzas, and indented lines in a way which forces the eye to move around the page to find connections, puzzlements and answers. Nevertheless, it could also stand as prose given the right context; little has been changed. Here are the first three lines of 'European Larch':

The Alps—
replaced by Norway Spruce
in colder, wetter areas—

This reformatting of prose in lines presents phrases that may not be intended in the original: 'Variants: 'Pendula', that / broad and depressed-looking tree displays / exaggeratedly weeping shoots', for example. The second line here describes 'Pendula' as depressed-looking but, cut from its original prose to stand alone, the line reads as a statement about displays of trees being depressed-looking. Using prose can thus allow a poem to emerge that suggests new meanings.

Many poets currently use prose as a source of a poem, as Morley has done; using syllabics offers one way to do so. While under no pressure to rewrite for rhythmic regularity, the poet can focus on the words that begin and end lines just as with any form of line, adjusting words to keep to the syllabic pattern. In practice, this process enhances my practice by revealing other meanings.

Similarly choosing syllabics to transform prose, W.D. Snodgrass said (p.25):

> I chose [the purely syllabic approach] for my poem, hoping it might open some new rhythmic possibilities to me, but hoping also that it would let me drop into occasional stretches of flat prose which might balance the rather "poetical" quality of the images I had collected.

This flattening of the register has intrigued poets as different as W.H. Auden and Philip Levine, and has been found useful in a variety of styles, from traditional lyrics such as Simon Armitage's 'Goalkeeper with a Cigarette' to radical conceptual offerings such as Kenneth Goldsmith's *No. 111.2.7.93 – 10.20.96/6,* which arranges transcribed texts by number of syllables. In Goldsmith's poem, entries of one syllable compose Chapter 1, two-syllable entries Chapter 2, etc. Raymond McDaniel, reviewing Goldsmith's work, regards this syllabic approach as 'obsessive' (p.367). This is a claim that could also be made about the usually well-regarded approaches of Oulipo, a group that believes constraint aids creativity. Of course all poems employ constraints, though the more usual ones might be less startling than, as Jacques Roubaud mentions in his surreal introduction to Oulipo, Jean Queval's invention of an alexandrine (a twelve-syllable iambic line) of variable length (Mathews, p.44). Oulipo promotes the use of number in poetry, and syllabic poetry is a straight-forward type of the poetry of number. A poet might well want to employ number for its rich symbolism as Sylvia Plath did in 'Metaphors', a nine-line poem about pregnancy, with nine syllables per line. It's not just to accommodate number that poets drop syllables from the beginning of words (apheresis) or the end (apocope) in ways once thought beautiful, but that can now sound excessively poetic. In a poem narrated by a pig going to the abattoir, Levine makes use of central syllable reduction (syncope) to suggest a socio-political reality (p.79):

> In my dreams
> the snouts drool on the marble
> suffering children, suffering flies,
>
> suffering the consumers
> who won't meet their steady eyes
> for fear they could see.

The word 'suffering' can be pronounced with either two or three syllables. Given the seven-syllable repeating line, the first two uses of 'suffering' must be two syllables and the third, three syllables. The word is thus drawn out in the final instance to enhance the irony on which the poem is founded: consumers, whose choice it is to eat pork and ignore animal and worker suffering, suffer more from moral shame. Consumers know pigs and workers must suffer in the creation of pork products for the market. The pigs suffer twice, but the word 'suffering' for them loses a syllable, twice, suggesting their suffering is a lesser thing. The line 'suffering the consumers' involves the consumers, alongside pigs and workers, in pain. How are consumers involved in suffering? While they create pain for pigs and workers, the line suggests, with its three-syllabled 'suff-er-ing' of the consumers, that the consumers are important in the market of meat-eaters to which pigs and workers must go. Their form of suffering is to bear the responsibility for the market conditions. Thus this poem, about capital and the relations of labour to the market, enhances its argument through its syllabics.

In this way, syllabics makes each word important as Rosellen Brown says of her book *Cora Fry* (Hammond, 1983):

> I chose syllabics as a form partly because that meant I would have to ration my words. They would be very dear, they would be very costly. Every time I wanted an adjective I would have to beg for it in my syllabic line.

Brown's assiduity, as suggested in this quotation, to the basic work of poetry, to make each word count in the poem's overall structure, is impressive. Rationing is an interesting metaphor to use with regard to syllabics; I see such necessary doling out of syllables, line by line, as one of the strengths of the method. Indeed, the word 'strength' is not, perhaps, thought of as an attribute of the syllabic approach because it seems so simple a sort of cut to make, from line to line; just stop your line when you get to eight, or eleven, or four, and see what happens. Of course, this is not how poets use syllabics. Moore, for example, exemplifies strength in her cold and cutting enjambments, while appearing to butcher the line arbitrarily. A line torn at 'on' or 'a', a word ripped into parts, syntax in pieces down a page: these syllabic executions of the line also give additional emphasis to the line ending. This is why I read many of Moore's syllabic poems as detached, clinical and ruthlessly dedicated to the final shape on the page.

There are other criticisms that one could make of the syllabic line. What is a syllabic line, for example, but an impure hybrid of irregular rhythm and ghosting metre? What does a stanza in contemporary syllabics sound like but an interstitial strophe? If we see those metrical descriptions as negative, then the syllabic poem is a good choice for a poem about a grotesque, horrifying or simply irregular subject. Michael Waters, for example, uses a ten-syllable line, characteristic of his work, to effect in 'Michelangelo Merisi Da Caravaggio – the Beheading of St John' (p.37):

> Tendons of the neck severed with the knife
> Still sheathed behind this executioner's
> Back – the beheading's not quite over yet,

Waters' use of syllabics stabilises horror with the inexorable control of each line. The line could go on, but it's not allowed. Given that it takes perhaps a third of a second to pronounce a syllable (whatever its length by letter) and three seconds constitutes the human auditory moment, as Frederick Turner and Ernst Pöppel have suggested, a ten-syllable line may be as much as one can process at once (Turner and Pöppel, p.286). Just when a reader can't take any more of the violence, the horrified brain pauses. Yet the horrifying number starts again, conscripting the reader. Syllabics proves a good choice for this interplay between meaningless neural experience and the build of painful imagery. After the first line gives a short shock, the second identical number of syllables delivers the killing thrust ending on 'gristly'. Expectation, delivered by metrical beat, might suggest hope in a hopeless world, but it is stripped away. The last line has nothing rhythmic to offer. These are cold formal attributes, reminiscent of human lack of emotion. Is syllabics here the psychopathy of the line, and is that why so many poets dislike it?

REFERENCES

Auden, W.H. (1972) *Academic Graffiti*. London: Random House.

Bridges, R. (1941) *Testament of Beauty*. Oxford: Clarendon Press.

Collard, D. (2013) *Bysshe. Rhymes with Sissy*. Available at: http://davidjcollard.blogspot.com/2013/01/bysshe-rhymes-with-sissy.html (Accessed: 18 February 2024).

Crapsey, A. (1922) *Verse*. New York, NY: Alfred A Knopf.

Daryush, E. (1921) *Sonnets from Hafez, and Other Verses*. British Library (Historical Print Editions undated). Oxford: Oxford University Press.

Daryush, E. (1972) *Selected Poems*. Manchester: Carcanet Press.

Davies, D. (1975) 'The Poetry of Elizabeth Daryush', *Poetry Nation* (5), pp.43-51.

Francis, M. (2001) *Dragons*. London: Faber and Faber.

Francis, M. (2015) Private communication with the author.

Ghose, Z. (1964) 'Defence of Syllabics', *Times Literary Supplement*, 3229, p.53.

Groves, P. (2013) 'Subversive Rhythms: Postcolonial Prosody and Indo-Anglian Poetry', *Thamyris/Intersecting*, (26), pp.123-124.

Gunn, T. (2017) *Selected Poems*. Edited by Wilmer, C. London: Faber and Faber.

Hall, D. and Lammon, M. (1993) *Flying Revision's Flag*. Available at: https://poets.org/text/flying-revisions-flag (Accessed: 18 February 2024).

Hammond, K.M. (1983) 'An Interview with Rosellen Brown', *Chicago Review*, 33 (3), pp.117-125. Available at: https://www.jstor.org/stable/25305181?origin=crossref (Accessed: 12 February 2024).

Johnson, B. S. (1964) *Poems*. London: Constable.

Levine, P. (1968) *Not This Pig*. Middletown, CT: Wesleyan University Press.

Mathews, H. (2005) 'Queval, Jean' in Mathews, H. and Brotchie, A. (eds.) *Oulipo Compendium*. London: Atlas Press, p.219.

McDaniel R. (2007) 'Affect and Autism: Kenneth Goldsmith's Reconstitution of Signal and Noise' in Rankine, C. and Sewell, L. (eds.) *American Poets in the 21st Century*. Middletown, CT: Wesleyan University Press, pp.367-381.

Mendelson, E. (1999) *Later Auden*. New York, NY: Farrar, Straus and Giroux.

Moore, M. (1982) *The Complete Poems of Marianne Moore*. London: Macmillan.

Moore, M. (1997) *Selected Letters*. London: Penguin.

Moore, M. (2017) *New Collected Poems*. London: Faber and Faber.

Morley, D. (2024) 'Creative Recognitions: Science, Writing and the Creative Academy'. Available at: https://www.liverpool.ac.uk/literature-and-science/archive/archiveofthepoetryandsciencehub/essays/creative-recognitions/ (accessed: 12 February 2024).

Needham, H.A. (undated) *Sidney, An Apology for Poetry, Shelley, A Defence of Poetry.* London: Ginn and Company.

Paz, O. (1973) *The Bow and the Lyre.* Translated by Ruth L.C. Simms. Austin, TX: University of Texas Press.

Plath, S. (1981) *Collected Poems.* London: Faber and Faber.

Shapcott, J. and Sweeney, M. (eds) (1996) *Emergency Kit: Poems for Strange Times.* London: Faber and Faber, pp.130-134.

Snodgrass, W.D. (1975) *In Radical Pursuit.* New York: Harper and Row.

Steele, T. (1999) *All the Fun's in How You Say a Thing.* Athens, OH: Ohio University Press.

Thomas, Dylan. (1987) *The Collected Letters.* Edited by Ferris, P. Boulder, CO: Paladin.

Thomas, Dylan. (1952) *Collected Poems.* London: J.M. Dent.

Turner, F. and Poppel, E. (1983) 'The Neural Lyre: Poetic Meter, the Brain, and Time'. *Poetry* 142 (5), pp. 277-309. Available at: https://www.jstor.org/stable/20599567 (Accessed: 12 February 2024).

Waters, M. (2011) *Gospel Night.* New York, NY: BOA Editions.

Collected Emotion

Denise Riley, *Say Something Back*

In the history of British attitudes to emotion, this century is no better than the nineteenth for making the tearful feel ashamed. A short way into Denise Riley's collection, *Say Something Back* (Picador, 2016), I gave in and cried at these words ('A Part Song, xv', p.13):

> The flaws in suicide are clear
> Apart from causing bother
> To those alive who hold us dear
> We could miss one another
> We might be trapped eternally
> Oblivious to each other
> One crying *Where are you, my child*
> The other calling *Mother.*

The sequence 'A Part Song' reflects on the sudden, shocking death of Riley's adult son. In the last line, 'The other calling *Mother*', his imagined shade has a chance (there are relatively few in this honest book) to say just the one loaded word, 'Mother'.

Riley is an historian of ideas and a postmodern poet well able to expose feelings in language. In *Impersonal Passion: Language as Affect*, she writes: 'If the affective quality of music can be granted to exist irrespective of its hearers' sensibilities and their quirks, then why not accord a similar relative independence to language's emotionality?' (2005, p.5). This implies that a poem delivers an emotional impact that is not caused by the meaningful words chosen by the poet, but that a reader can come to a poetic work, as they could to a melody, and be emotionally entertained, enlightened even. She exemplifies the affective quality of language in this collection, a devastating performance of rant, sob and whisper ('After 'Nous n'irons plus au bois', p.33):

> We've had it with the woods.
> The underbrush got felled.
> Grab who you want, now

The title of the poem refers to an old French children's song, traditionally sung to a chant from the Latin Mass of the Angels, once an everyday mass and sometimes used to elegise a child's death. Poetry lovers may also enjoy the demolition of the elegant eighteenth-century line, 'The Poplars are fell'd, farewell to the shade' from William Cowper's 'The Poplar-Field' (p.67). There are many other emotions attributed to language in these poems. Hear the longing, the hope even in these lines from 'Listening for Lost People': 'The souls of the dead are the spirit of language: / you hear them alight inside that spoken thought' (p.32). Poetry, despair says, is a way to meet again.

Apart from the affect of language itself, Riley's thoughts form the memory of experience, as all memories must be formed. Her poems describe that painful experience, as here in 'And another thing' (p.37):

> Does sifting through damage ease, or enshrine it; how grasp
> a past, but not skid on embittered accounting? The ledgers
> exhibit their black surplus malice and red lack of tenderness,
> while 'suffering' easily gets competitive as each suspects hers
> was the rougher lot

The experience of loss and death is no less a puzzle despite its incontrovertibility, she suggests here, and thinking back evokes unpleasant emotions, 'embittered accounting' and 'surplus malice'.

Riley has not been a prolific poet, having lurched, as she has put it, between verse and philosophy or critical work during a long writing career. In an essay, *Time Lived, Without Its Flow* (Picador, 2019), she refers particularly to her sense that time stopped for two years after her son's death (Baraitser, 2020, online):

> What I thought was that of all those millions of people in the world who for one reason or another, some infinitely more violent and distressing than others, find themselves outliving their children, a range of reactions and emotions, some of which might be easily describable, some of which may not be, some of which may be predictable, and some of which may be anarchic and terrifying, or even blackly comic, if I, just one tiny sliver, make a stab at speaking about it, then it may be of some interest, or even some consolation, though that might be a bit over-ambitious on my part.

The detail in this one long sentence is anguished; again, language, grammar and choice of adverb and noun ('blackly', 'stab') help Riley to convey emotion. There is a progression from an initial attempt to give perspective to the death of a grown child, from analytic ('for one reason or another') through anxious muttering ('some of which…some of which… some of which') to a defeated apology ('might be a bit over-ambitious on my part'). The narrator sounds desperate.

Say Something Back's very title urges a spoken response from the dead, and demanding imperatives recur in the poems: 'Come home I tell you…' ('A Part Song, vii', p.8), 'Get away with you now' ('With Child in Mind', p.30). The title of the collection wheedles as well as orders as here in 'A Part Song, xix' (p.14):

> For the point of this address is to prod
> And shepherd you back within range
> Of my strained ears; extort your reply…

The first line, a reference to T.S. Eliot's 'The Waste Land', allows Riley's narrator to act the mad mother, but then she explains that she does so 'to prod… you back' and '[to] extort your reply'. The collection's title phrase, 'say something back', is not an imperative (it comes from the book's epigraph, by W.S. Graham); the change in grammatical use allows Riley's narrator to act the child and also the magician, the magus, the mad mother, to bluster like an ineffectual bully and to construct human emotion in a postmodern way, with the texts of other poets' struggles ringing in her lines. 'A Part Song, xv' (p.12) illustrates this superbly. It adapts the ending of George Herbert's seventeenth-century masterpiece, 'The Collar' (p.524):

> But as I rav'd and grew more fierce and wild
> At every word
> Me thought I heard one calling Childe!
> And I reply'd My Lord.

Riley's lines are equally powerful:

> We might be trapped eternally
> Oblivious to each other

One crying *Where are you my child*
The other calling *Mother.*

In the eighteenth century, John and Charles Wesley (leaders of the Wesleyan movement) adapted 'The Collar', and their hymn picks out Herbert's last two lines to set up a repeating quatrain, ballad fashion. Herbert varied the rhythm of lines throughout his poem, but finished confidently on a three-beat line. Riley allows the sing-along style to float her poem, but gives every second line three-and-a-half beats, a usefully weaker feminine line ending than those second lines stomping through the hymn's verses. Having summoned up male poet mentors, she rewrites them with the negative force of her twenty-first-century sensibility and thus slips, semantically and rhythmically, out of comforting Christianity into a faltering last line. Riley replaces Herbert's triumphant shout to his immortal parent with a hopeless echo from the 'other'.

More hymns, literary tropes, and myths recur through the collection to illuminate the guilt of surviving one's child. In 'Orphic', an ironic take on the Orpheus story, a newly dead mother encounters her long-dead son, who reproaches her for the bewailing she has done while he has had to endure death: 'I've lived here dead for decades – now you / pitch up gaily among us shades, with your / freshly dead face all lit up, beaming…' (p.34). He needs her, though: 'So mother / do me proud and hold your white head high'. Eurydice here is a dead son stuck in Hades; Orpheus is the living parent who has had to walk away from loss, and here s/he is, back at last, thrilled to be with him again and thus presenting Riley's experience in another moving illustration of the extremity of such a bereavement.

In 'Cardiomyopathy', referring to her son's heart condition, Riley indicts the surviving parent's heart for its odious failure to stop beating (p.55):

> *My living on indicts me. If my own heart*
> *contracted briefly, it still pushed on past yours.*
>
> *Hearts, being muscular, power on as they can.*
> *Mine was relentless in outpacing yours.*

This book does not offer the usual elegy, as the poet swerves from the easier path of meeting her own need for comfort. Under the severe psychic stress of losing a child, Riley manages her poetics with her usual philosophical rigour and even wit.

REFERENCES

Baraitser, L. and Riley, D. (2020) 'Lisa Baraitser in Conversation with Denise Riley', *Feminist Theory*, 21 (3), pp. 339-349. Available at doi: https://doi.org/10.16995/sim.206 (Accessed: 29 January 2024).

Herbert, G. (2010) *The English Poems of George Herbert*. Cambridge: Cambridge University Press.

Rhodes, N. (ed) (2003) *Selected Poems: William Cowper*. Manchester: Fyfield Books at Carcanet Press.

Riley, D. (2005) *Impersonal Passion: Language as Affect*. Durham, NC: Duke University Press.

Riley, D. (2016) *Say Something Back*. London: Picador.

Riley, D. (2019) *Time Lived, Without Its Flow*. London: Picador.

Cracking the Geode

Jean 'Binta' Breeze, *The Verandah Poems*
Michael Symmons-Roberts, *Selected Poems*

Looking into Jean 'Binta' Breeze's eighth collection *The Verandah Poems* surprised me, so drab do I expect poetry books to be: a title page with red and green letters and Tehron Royes's richly-coloured photos scattered through the text. The pictures amplify vivid stories in the poems, journalling Breeze's return to Jamaica, where she grew up, and her recuperation from illness there. She has written them on the verandah of her childhood home, as the title suggests: a place to sit and observe the sea, the sky and the community, and to think about the changes in Hillside, the family house backing the verandah, bequeathed to her by her grandmother Sheba.

As she sits writing in this colonial setting, Jean, the narrator, is asked by passersby for sex, money, and her thoughts on old and new ways. Bush medicine, for example, is a contentious subject, and Breeze shows the differing points of view in 'Evening' (p.19):

Phillip is into bush
for his nerves
it's sour sop leaf tea
neem is the cure for diabetes
and the present miracle bush is called
merengeh
He chews the seed
and drinks the leaves in hot tea
every morning

My mother passes by that bit of talk
on her way to water flowers in the front garden
'I will die of something I'm sure
but I won't die of bush,' she says

The debates about Jean's homeland bear down on one question for her: to go back to the UK or stay in Jamaica. There are pressures to go, such as the intense heat. Family arguments reflect a climate of heat and storms in 'Heat' (p.44):

> By lunch time
> if we're lucky
> the thunder of the early afternoon
> will break the sky
> and the rain smell of the earth
> will cool us humans down
> and maybe
> just maybe
> night will not come
> with the anger
> of heated arguments

Staying in Jamaica is attractive, too. 'Stranger' is a moving life-story told, in the poem, by a beggar. In the UK, such a stranger might not be welcomed, but he is free to come onto Jean's verandah because this is 'countryside Jamaica', and here he is welcomed and allowed to tell his story. The man can beg with dignity (p.16):

> so just a bus fare
> for not every man is a dawg
> no mam
> not every man is a dawg
> if you have children
> you know what I mean
> not every man is a dawg
>
> He leaves me on the verandah
> leaves with my last fifty dollars
> leaves me
> with the two sides of the story

Breeze has written previously of her early life and Sheba's, notably in *The Fifth Figure*. That remarkable *tour de force*, in my view her major work, examined the historic mix of white and black people in Jamaica, and the disruption and pain of living in a society of clashing cultures. *The*

Verandah Poems is a quieter book, smaller in scope and pitch perfect in tone and form as in 'A Visit from Scotland' (p.33):

> This rastaman
> I do not recognise
> but from the confidence of his step
> he recognises me
>
> Sista Breeze
> yuh come?

That journey to adulthood is made by us all. Hers is not a simple trip, from Jamaica to England, warm to cold, village familiarity to spoken word icon. Breeze's narratives illuminate both cultures, Caribbean and English, by creating a palimpsest, illuminating one with the other, as in her earlier poem, 'The Wife of Bath in Brixton Market', engagingly performed to camera in Brixton Market itself. Breeze is a seasoned performer, and *The Verandah Poems* works as well aurally as on the page (pp.35-37):

> I am about to put the first bite in my mouth
> when my stepfather looks at me deeply
> Jean, he says,
> 'if you should die in England
> do you want to be buried there,
> or shall we bring home your body?'
>
> [...]
>
> bring nothing home I say
> cremate
> on the spot
> and if you want
> spread the dust across the sea
> I belong to the wind and to the sea
> not to worms
> or roots of trees

These poems are plain writing on the surface but filled with coruscating experience; geodes, worth cracking open.

Michael Symmons Roberts's *Selected Poems* is an extended piece of mystical writing. This overpowering collection has no sections, through 163 pages and twenty years of poetry. Yet the poems show us splits as well as joins, from the first ('Angel of the Perfumes', p.1):

> From the night-shift cement works,
> dust built on fields, seeped
> into buildings, coughed me awake.

Here are Roberts's favourite scenarios: deadly night, creation's day of the woken soul, the world as we know it, the world as the narrator believes it to be, an otherworldly being shortly to come to a human narrator (an angel in stanza four). The spiritually sensitive poems, ordinary in descriptive detail, are also transfigured. And they are witty ('Food for Risen Bodies V', p.80):

> He turned down the banquet
> – broth to brie – '*Later, later*'

Metaphors used in mystical writing occur through the book: the abyss, for example ('Abyss of Birds', p.154):

> It begins in song, in fact in songs, such chaos
> it's as if each dead bird is reborn to join
> the same dawn chorus

Canonical poets homaged by Roberts (Hopkins, Donne) use the natural world to exemplify the divine. Roberts sees God in the edgelands (he has co-written an award-winning book on these inbetween boundaries to our settlements) and in the city ('Night Drive', p.96):

> No evening cool, no garden. A metropolis.
> The dead hours. Air steams with sleepers.
>
> Empty streets, slow between sheer glass,
> no one expects him to come like this.

This poem refigures Jesus for our time. Aside from mysticism, which can strike a believer of any religion, many of the poems' narratives are ghosts of Biblical tales. Roberts was an atheist, an aggressive one he says, and is now a Catholic. I grew up in that culture and love to spot a lurking Catholic plot, but I wonder how it reads for someone not already familiar with these stories. Can an atheist appreciate the countless references to 'soul'? Roberts 'biblicises' the apparently godless: nuclear power, war, genetic life ('Origin of Species', p.108).

> so cold they held each other tight
> beneath the leaves for warmth.
>
> ...   There is nothing here to mark
>
> this as the place where humankind began,
> just the embers of a fire nearby,
>
> still smouldering, a pair of jeans, some tee
> shirts dripping on a branch...

Poets can transfigure a myth into a contemporary observation; we look around and are exhilarated. This is wonderfully and lightly done in 'Annunciation at the Hookses' (p.4):

> O Gabriel make her waking as gentle
> as the eye-blue of a distant sail.
> Still she'll drop her half-full glass
> in shock and joy at what you ask.

The reader sees divine union with the clever insertion of divine absence in 'half-full glass'. The phrase 'shock and joy' suggests an absent word, 'awe', which would have been appropriate in this spiritual context if the phrase had not been famously appropriated by the military.

I enjoy the sequences in this selection (Roberts has included four), perhaps because they offer some ordering of the lyric onslaught. *Selected Poems* is, in a way, one long sequence, a sustained examination of how souls spend their human term, as illustrated in 'The Frequency' (p.87):

> Night falls now,
> and under lightlessness I listen

for the footfalls of God in the garden.
The cool of evening is the time

he walked beneath the boughs of Eden,
softly, with his lips dried shut.
The apple was gone, man and woman
with it, and already

the bass tones of birdsong
were becoming shrill, sonorities
of breeze in grass were turning
into whispers. This was the fall of sound,

a rise in frequency which rendered paradise
inaudible.

Roberts's stance in this book is, if not missionary, nevertheless deeply convinced of a world some readers don't live in. Thus his beliefs are his weakness as well as his strength, a peculiarly Christian position. Be aware rather than beware of his exquisitely written poetry.

REFERENCES

Breeze, J.B. (2016) *The Verandah Poems*. Hexham: Bloodaxe Books.
Roberts, M.S. (2016) *Selected Poems*. London: Jonathan Cape.

Polish That Thought

Joanne Limburg, *The Autistic Alice*
Fran Lock, *Dogtooth*
Shara McCallum, *Madwoman*

Are words responsible for reality as well as representing it? Do they create their own reality that is separate from everyday life as well as making a poetic picture of life? Joanne Limburg examined this question meticulously in her prose memoir, *The Woman Who Thought Too Much* (Atlantic, 2011), and takes it up again in her new collection, *The Autistic Alice* (Bloodaxe, 2017), in 'Alice's Un-Birthday' (p.32):

'I'm four,' she says.

'No, you're not,' her mother says,
[...]
It isn't saying it that makes it true.

A child's bewilderment and anger flash through this poem and the whole book. Like Stevie Smith, Limburg knows how to convey those feelings formally. 'Brother' (p.11), for example, ends with the exasperated line: 'For pity's sake, pick up'. When you know that the narrator is pleading with her brother to respond from the dead, the anger becomes part of the grieving process, enriching the sense of feeling in that line.

Just as Limburg's children's collection, *Bookside Down* (Salt, 2013), is sharp enough for adult readers, some of these poems would work for older children. The Alice poems, for example, with their depiction of autism couched in imagery from *Alice in Wonderland* and *Alice Through the Looking Glass*: a pack of cards, a tiger lily, a chess board, and two queens. These poems present the longest and strongest section of three in the collection. 'Other Poems', the final set, is an assortment of bleakly funny poems, creating magnificent metaphors reminiscent of Selima Hill ('The View from Crieff', p.69):

...mountains like mauve dowagers,
[...] glowering indigo matrons

The first section, 'The Oxygen Man' (published as a pamphlet in 2012), is a harrowing account of the immediate aftermath of Limburg brother's death by suicide. In 'Brother' (p.11), Limburg patterns the poem tightly, using one word ('name') as an epistrophe, perhaps the better to control emotion:

> ... we nearly shared a name.

> Now I'm Joanne, alone, and call your name.

At the memorial service, Limburg is embarrassed by her own jokes ('Double Act', p.18):

> ...Posthumously, my brother wowed,

> and so, accepting the honour as his sister,
> I had to say, 'And I thought it was only
> a career move for poets.' Laughter,

> at this, was slight, and centre stage was lonely.

Her first collection *Femenismo* (Bloodaxe, 2000) established a defiant voice with humour that also lightens the emotional claustrophobia of *The Autistic Alice* ('The Loft Day', p.63):

> I felt pushed to express it all,
> [...]
> and when my mother just went '*What?*
> I realised she wasn't *feeling* it.

The poem shows us what it is like to feel differently: words have meanings, the narrator says, that are not 'understood but *felt*: / they mean like a colour in a painting'. The narrator feels different to her family and feels differently, in a different manner to them. Different feelings can be embarrassing or guilt-inducing (though why should they be?): 'To be alive is to be embarrassed, / a helpless source of mistakes and smells.' ('A Run Round All Souls', p.65). Discomfort is essential to most of Limburg's work, but if the poems do cause us discomfort, perhaps we need to know not just our most embarrassing features but, more importantly, what cruelties we inflict. These poems raise awareness of our complicity in the social pain suffered by what Limburg calls the 'awkward one' ('Queen Alice', p.55).

For a rant made out of steel, read Fran Lock's third collection, *Dog-tooth* (Out-Spoken Press, 2017). Imagine wail after wail cooled and hammered into lyric lines ('Cop car, burning', p.40):

> ...I
> am filled with sad directionless
> tenderness. And I am filled by
> a drab grace that clutches straws,
> and I have had it up to my ears
> with the scream that we suffer
> like a stone in the mouth. *Your* filth,
> *your* fear, *your* blame.

Lock resists the accommodations most of us make to what she calls 'obliteration and affront' (p.41). If it is normal to accept, for example, what she calls 'the galloping / wretchedness of age' (p.41), Lock's narrator will not. To indicate resistance, the narrator swears – 'shit-bag' (p.9), 'fuck it' (p.41), 'sodding daffodils' (p.46), 'fucking panpipes' (p.46) – or rushes into a description of social or civic surroundings, packed with adjectives, as in this passage from 'My social media presence' (p.50):

> I like the hellbent
> hiccuping flight of pigeons, the rag
> and bone genetics of mongrel dogs;
> toast, and the steely shrinking radiance
> of city skies.

This poem explores a social persona; the society she inhabits is one suffering poverty. The poor (and the aged and political extremists), many poems suggest, exist among us like ghosts. Her untitled foreword to the collection starts in a child's voice (p.6):

> My friend wants to know what the book's about. ...I don't like
> being put on the spot, and she's looking at me like she's trying
> to explode my head with her mind. I bite my nails and squirm

in my seat and blurt out the first thing that comes to me: *It's about ghosts.*

The foreword later assumes an intellectual, adult, tone: 'Yes, ghosts…as in the discomforts, paranoias and phobias that haunt a very particular cultural moment' (p.6). This sums up Lock's usual choice of topics. She can write about drugs and violence as if reality played out through the 1960s films of Franco Fellini, in the city streets alongside the poor. Here she summons up suburbia (specifically the London borough of Sutton) in a collage of jargons ('Uplinked real-time nonversation', p.8):

> …Goddaughters
> glitching like microbes, cybertising Brides
> of Christ, textperts savvying word blobs
> with swasticky fingers. The gang's all
> here: feral prelates, pit-bull dogs. Ford
> Cortina is a Spinning Jenny – a moody
> ethnic relic, phosphorating green.

The imagery here is as vivid as the adjectives and participles, 'swasticky', 'cybertising'. Unpredictably, these technicolour lines bring me into the wild life described. Indeed, it is a rare poet who can make me feel personally addressed when she uses the second person, even though it's obvious the narrator is not talking to the reader ('The ghost in you', p.54):

> …I dance with you. In dreams.
> And you are drunk, I think, and in a lisping
> vein. My hair's the brittle and teetering pink
> of fairgrounds. I do not recognize myself. I
> dance with you.

There is a desperation to describe throughout Lock's work and a sense, as she says in the lines above, that the poet never quite recognises the ghosts, those people and situations she finds in her descriptions. Nor has she beaten into submission the squads of adjectives that bothered her previous collection ('Under the boardwalk', p.24):

> …A red buoy is a wound in
> the carbon scarf of the sea. And we are dazzled meat on such

a bluely bulging day as this. *Boardwalk*. liquefied folly in
paper cups.

While some of these overwrought poems can be difficult to read, they
present the hard and scary work of living in a striking, convincing
way. If *Dogtooth* is not such a roller-coaster as Lock's last collection,
The Mystic and the Pig Thief, it forges something impressive from our
corrupted times.

Poets have used many devices to present the complex of personality.
Shara McCallum revivifies personification in her new, fifth collection,
Madwoman (Peepal Tree, 2017). Red, Death, and Grief, for example,
are personifications that strut their colour and emotion in retellings of
Jamaican and North American fairy tales and fabulous family legends. In
'Grief', 'When I hover, you hear cicadas crescendo. / You mistake me for
winter's onset / or the body as it ages. Foolish girl.' (p.70). However low
key the delivery, personifications such as Red and Grief seem grandiose,
and they put McCallum's often epiphanic endings under pressure.

To whom are these personifications – these bits of our selves – talking?
McCallum establishes a listener in the pseudo character, Madwoman.
There has been a feminist free-for-all with this fictional Everywoman,
before and since Jane Eyre's alter ego in the attic. In a long and impressive
final poem, McCallum's Madwoman floats between questions and her
own answers in a song-like catechism ('Madwoman Apocrypha', p.71). It
begins:

> *When comes the night that made you?*
>
>   In this field: snow not yet underfoot,
> trees whose branches are shorn of leaves,
>   this sky a grey slate over and around
> houses echoing the shape of the river,
>
> Q: What created you?
> A: A breach in the self.

The poem (and the collection) ends with an affirmation of the power of
poetry to materialise desire: 'Say *bird* and it will trill or twitter or even
sing' (p.77). The narrator absorbed this understanding early: 'When as a
child words found me', and that was 'the night of [her] unmaking' (p.77).

Madness and poetry, beautifully expressed in the phrase 'a breach in the self', are linked here as they have been in other cultures at other times.

McCallum has said in an interview: 'In poems, I am often drawn to areas and moments in our lives where the self appears to come apart' (McCallum, 2021). However, McCallum's poems consider a maddening world with calm and clarity. Her analysis of these moments in *Madwoman* is not that of actual mental illness; instead, they offer a guide into a stylized space in which to consider the broken or multiple self.

REFERENCES

Limburg, J. (2017) *The Autistic Alice*. Hexham: Bloodaxe Books.

Lock, F. (2017) *Dogtooth*. London: Out-Spoken Press.

McCallum, S. (2017) *Madwoman*. Leeds: Peepal Tree.

McCallum, S. (2021) 'Five Questions with Shara McCallum'. Available at: https://m.facebook.com/NatureIslandLiteraryFestival/posts/five-questions-with-shara-mccallum-5-catherine-clement-in-opera-or-the-undoing-o/10158178636543697/ (Accessed: 24 December 2023).

Senior, O. (1988) 'To The Madwoman in My Yard', *Callaloo* 36. Avail-able at: https://doi.org/10.2307/2931527 (Accessed: 24 December 2023).

Fabulous Facts

Sasha Dugdale, *Joy*
Sina Queyras, *My Ariel*

Joy (Carcanet, 2017), Sasha Dugdale's fourth collection, escorts the reader through displacements, disavowals, and the destructive forces of history. Here are lines from 'How my friend went to look for her roots' (p.46):

> This little town had an ancient centre, but nowhere to eat. The
> little hotel was shut for repairs a thousand years
> in the completing, and the woman who poked her head from a
> window said:
>
> –If you're from here then why don't you stay with your family?
>
> –My family left.
>
> So, asked the woman, why come here then?

These lines bring to mind the Rip Van Winkle story, suggesting that fable is where facts start. Dugdale's poem 'The Canoe', about the making of local fables, could be an oral poem delivered on an Anglo-Saxon winter's night. After beloved community members have sailed away, those left behind have become resentful and destroyed the empty homes of their lost friends (p.38):

> So who can blame the ones who broke in and stole
> Who brought on the collapse, by breaking in doors and
>   windows
> Who fell about in a wild frenzy then, and drove at ceilings,
>   boards
> With hooked poles, hoping for treasures to come pouring forth.
> Then, encouraged by the fierce and glorious joy of destruction
> They cudgelled chairs with chair legs, tossed cups like coconuts
> Stamped and urinated and spat at the walls in spasms
> Of horror…

This long free-verse poem, declaimed by a bard, implies the dispersal during war as well as in travel and language. Forced displacements described in received forms, such as the ballad, sonnet and villanelle, lull the reader into facing horror. 'Ironing the Spider' is a poem whose title conveys its irony. 'My most violent act: once ironing a spider,' says the narrator, adding 'I can't abide violence.' Subsequently, the spider rears up, a 'meaty widow' (p.42):

> I have since seen her soul all scorched and resentful
> Her spirit crushed and oozing. I am reminded then
> Of the railway victims on the Pskov station board.
> It read: do you recognize these men?

Dugdale's unruffled tone makes the gender bias of historic victimhood more piercing. The long title poem 'Joy' is a nuanced feminist depiction of Catherine Blake, wife of William Blake and fellow artist (p.12):

> I remember how you taught me many things. When I met you
> a thousand years ago and that is not extravagant because you
> knew how to press on time and release it from its skin to grow
> you knew that about time and all manner of other wisdoms
> and how to release the sky from the indignant thistle, and col-
> our from powder and line from copper and sense from letters
> which danced like demons on the page.

The poem is an intense lyrical outpouring from a woman close to death as well as a compelling drama. Yet it has an occasional eerie quality, as in the final lines of the quote above. These poems are compelling stories of strange happenings in an almost imperceptibly strange style.

Canadian poet Sina Queyras's *My Ariel* (Coach House, 2017) pulses with anger, the characteristic feeling in Sylvia Plath's final, posthumous work. The long poem 'Years', composed of quotes from Plath's journals and letters as well as other texts about Plath, exemplifies this (p.51):

> > > > > *Ariel* is a burst,
> A big fuck you to the corset, why bang back on domesticity's
> Door? The poem, the poem, it's not pastoral at all, it's war,
> War, war.

My Ariel, confessional in approach, as Queyras integrates her own life and poetry with Plath's, offers a thorough examination of how Queyras's vocation as a poet has survived becoming a parent ('The Bee Meeting', p.111):

> Babies sleep under my tongue. Quiet now,
> I must rest my mind, surround myself
> With creamy Amazons, those I have glimpsed
> Through strips of tinfoil winking like crows – no,
> No, you cannot eat my heart, I have wrapped
>
> My organs, stacked my selves in sleeves
> Of muslin: one of me must survive. One of me
> Must live on between the lines.

Phrases such as 'those I have glimpsed' and 'one of me' suggest the strange doubling effect of a later poet channelling a former and famous poet. However, at double the length of *Ariel*, *My Ariel* feels overlong: Queyras uses poem after poem from *Ariel*, often with the same titles to describe the guilt, frustration and eventual absolution of parents. She shows how the narrator's mother inadvertently killed a child, how Ted Hughes deals with Plath's death for the rest of his life, and how the narrator drifts, guilt-fogged, into the male parental role, sidelined by her partner giving birth ('In the Birth Canal', p.125):

> I am not who I thought I would be in this situation. I cannot
>   recognize myself at all. I am all shortcomings. All lack.
> I pace. Wait. Go in search of a vending machine. In the elevator
>   there are no forceps. I think, This must be an oversight.
> A young man with a mop and pail sits in a corridor filled with
>   discarded medical equipment texting and talking by Blue
>   tooth.
> Ted was with you for both births. My father caught me. I am
>   observing myself observe.

Queyras's own struggle with parenthood shows in the last, most dynamic section of the book, an account of the poet's final push not so much away from the dominance of the mother as toward acceptance of her own gender-conflicted parenthood. 'Tribes of Mommies Just Like You' claims writing as the way forward (p. 146):

> Apparently there are tribes of mommies who think like men and
> tribes of men who think like mommies. Elsewhere there are
> writers who move fluidly through these modes. I am on the
> lookout. I am watching pronouns foam at the wake.

Ending the volume on her own version of 'Ariel' and a positive note
of ongoing parenthood and poethood compares with Plath's original
ordering of *Ariel* ending with 'Wintering,' a hopeful poem about spring
coming. Queyras acknowledges the strength of all parents, including the
female one burgeoning inside herself (p.152):

> My love hauls
>
> Me up. She is still here,
> Beside me. We float on a white
> Sea, Sylvia, where the dead
>
> Make themselves particulars
> That hang together
> And form something firm
>
> As flanks; steps
> Of joy that, like the hours,
> We master and release.

'We float on a white / sea, Sylvia...' both addresses Sylvia and suggests
that Sylvia is the sea, a dead sea that supports the weight of future parents.
My Ariel is a reminder that motherhood can be as much a linguistic as a
biological activity. More, poems can procreate: the fruitful relationship
between Queyras's creativity and Plath's poetry has given birth to new
poems and contributed to Plath's afterlife.

REFERENCES

Dugdale, S. (2018) *Joy*. Manchester: Carcanet Press.
Queyras, S. (2017) *My Ariel*. Toronto: Coach House Books.

Shattered Idylls

Beverley Bie Brahic, *The Hotel Eden*
Kit Fan, *As Slow As Possible*
and Amy Key, *Isn't Forever*

The Hotel Eden is Beverley Bie Brahic's fourth book of poetry (she has also published sixteen books of prose and poetry translations), a cool collection of fragmentary minidramas. The title poem, acknowledging Joseph Cornell, a pioneer of assembly art, explains the value of scraps: 'From laughter to slaughter the house of objects is repossessed' (p.13). Scraps may seem dull, ('Butt-end of an egg. / The spring from a gutted clock'), but the poet can enhance them (p.13):

On the tip of God's tongue, the bird waits to be named.

That tough attitude transforms many of the poems' scenes into standoffs. Brahic shows some lovely thing – the reflection of the moon, six jars of honey – but then sounds irritated with her lush visuals, as in 'Land's End' (p.76):

We sniff the grass that smells
Fresh cut, watch the brides'
Stiletto heels stab porous turf.
The spires of the Golden Gate
Rise through a frieze
Of cypress trees

These verbs, 'cut' and 'stab', nip at the idyll, as do judgments, such as the anti-classical jibe, '*Vita brevis* days are long', until the last line, which presents as romantic but seems to crawl with irritation: 'The light is consecrating everything.' 'The Lady and the Hollyhock' describes bucolic pleasure, 'a pretty vision' (p.44), which develops a sour taste. The last lines spit bathos: 'Underneath a gargoyle / Who's just a water spout.'

The first poem, 'Madame Martin and I', depicts an old couple spraying roses and pegging out sheets, an idyllic scene till the speaker viciously dispatches one of the pair in the final stanza (p.11):

He was sick all of a sudden
He was dead
And now he's gone
She says she thinks she hardly knew him.

Reversing that nice-to-nasty shock, in the final poem, 'The Back Road', the speaker finds only shade and mud on her route home so changes her path and, at last, sees unappreciated beauty: 'Beside a slope of gently blazing vineyards / where *grappillons* still hang – / Grapes for the gleaners' (p.80). How menacing is the verb 'hang'? Is 'blazing' ever a gentle adjective? Grappillons are late grapes, more acidic than earlier bunches, but still picked and enjoyed. This poem is a hiker's view of cemetery and shade, a reminder of death and, with that perspective, we can look back on the whole collection as building towards a feeling of nightmare, where laughter becomes slaughter, and Brahic's photographic scrutiny of objects and experiences darkens.

As *Slow As Possible*, Kit Fan's second collection, flies through eras and cultures. In 'A Chair from Buddha Mountain', a chair, made in one cultural and geographical setting, is designed to be sold in a very different place (p.40):

I was born in the seventh year of the second millennium
up the Pearl River Delta in the city of Foshan – Buddha

Mountain – where two-thirds of the world's chairs are born
every year in my hometown. I belong to the family of patio

chairs, a tough, durable breed made to withstand the Cretan
sun and Aberdeenshire gales.

This international mobility is borne out by Fan's life; a biographical note reads: 'As his poetry moves between Hong Kong and European cultural histories, he moves amphibiously between poetry and narrative fiction' (p.81). As suggested by the 'tough, durable breed' of chairs, Fan is interested in the way history and the organic world and, indeed, migrants, survive. He describes spring in reverse in 'Resistance': 'There comes a time a leaf will furl back to its vein / with generations of green mouths unbudding / as a form of protest, a way of branching in' (p.27). Similarly, 'Anatomical and Human Sciences' runs through eras of medical development, via Genesis, Galen, Mascagni, and *Gray's Anatomy* to our time, describing the poet's childhood experience of medical examination. Fan conveys this progression more generally as 'a generation of green mouths / passes secret messages to one another / like Chinese whispers.' (p.32). If Fan is a Mercury, flying with winged poetic heels from era to era, he is relaxed about it ('Les Alyscamps', p.23):

> We saunter
>> through the road of open tombs, unnamed
>> by their weathered stones. Here a trace of Adam hiding
>> in the leaves and there a firstborn dangling
>> from a sword. Christ was here once, attending a funeral.

This description of a French necropolis, where Gauguin and Van Gogh painted together, encompasses a long history, from Genesis to the Christian era, while the poem focuses on a friend or relative accompanying the poet through the outward signs of Death, graves and dust: 'what returns to the ground returns / to dust.'

The geography of Fan's poems continually gives way to rupture. Many of the poems contain such negative words as 'not', 'no', 'without', and 'nothing'. Fan often uses such negatives to set a scene, as in 'Breughel's Trees': 'There was a time when we were not here. / Not stirring the primal scene, not stealing the thunder / from some god' (p.45). Anaphora hammers the negatives in 'To the Shadow-Millions' (p.25):

> What do the shadows remember?
> Not the fireworks.
> Not the laser beams.
> Not the moth in fire chasing its own shadow.

Fan acknowledges here the 'shadow-millions' whose lives are affected by the darkness of political realities. With its lost civilisations, its many negatives, and even tired phrases such as 'nothing at all' ('The Burning of Books'), this collection is a dream of negative thought. It reminds us that we will be lost, whether through death, planetary extinction, or the destructive effects of social injustice. The final poem achieves an exquisite rendition of last moments, including those that will be reborn and renewed in a new year, as Fan underlines by using an epigraph from Emily Dickinson: 'Forever is deciduous – / except to those who die'.

Humans and leaves disappear in the cycle Fan evokes so well through this collection; nevertheless, it's particularly brave, I think, to finish a collection with 'a yearlong full stop / rounding on and off December' (p.74), as if there is nothing more to say. But Fan adds one more thing: below the last poem is a list of Farrow and Ball paint colours in shades of white followed by a quote from Richard II: 'Each substance of a grief hath twenty shadows'. Those are two different approaches to light and shadow, one literary and the other, while imaginative, aimed at a buying, rather than a reading, consumer. Putting them together adds an unexpected context to the poem above them. The paint shades appear in the poem as the 'substance of a nothing', surely a good way to describe paint.

There are many ways to be negative in poetry, and Amy Key's way, in her second collection *Isn't Forever*, is sassy. From the title on, her demeanour says 'take me or leave me, you'll have to leave me anyway, and I'm dealing with it'. 'I do not need the sea to love me back' provides one example (Key, 2018, p.12). The poem ends 'I waited for the sea to notice me / ~~But the sea never notices anyone~~'. This poem of statements, many of them one-liners, reads simply, but the collection makes many more complex attempts to call attention to the speaker, as in 'Announcement and next steps' (p.13):

In the absence of anything as definitive
as blood type or maths, I am delighted to declare
I found the back to the earring, also the mildew is banished,
albeit temporarily. I want to share this news with you,
a check against the inventory of living. Personalised
necklaces point to living. Customisable anything suggests it's all
worth it.

The opening sentence of the passage accrues many dependent clauses. This voice sounds very different to the conversational one in the first quotation; this speaker declaims to an audience. She tries to make the reader laugh at her bathos: 'also the mildew is banished / albeit temporarily.' One of Key's techniques is to mix confessed ignorance with the wisdom of aphorisms, such as 'The boundaries between self-sabotage / and self-nourish have never been murkier' ('She lacks confidence…', p.30) and 'The heart is permanently gory' ('The Best Is Yet to Come', p.65). Some sayings appear familiar, while some quote from other writers: 'Only instead of a star' (p.35) is a cento that includes the purposefully awful line 'everything seems very awful' from Key's great-great-aunt Mabel's diary. The variety of forms and typography is exhilarating, appearing gappy, slashed, sectioned, in columns, and in prose. Key conveys her downtrodden persona's emotional frustration in grand-sounding lines in 'The Best Is Yet to Come' (p.67):

> I have forgiven the lies I've been told that were intended to
>   soothe me.

>   ~

> My enterprise has been: an attempt
> to force emotion from things.

>   ~

> Feelings often lack structural integrity –

> we're all falling into each other.

>   ~

> My feelings can't afford the plans I'm making.

These passages show a mature grasp of human awfulness, forgiving lies, analysing feelings, and observing human behaviour while accepting its continual neediness. As I noted at the start of this review, Key's focus is human foibles, and she describes them from the title on. Few collections enjoy titles as much as this one does, from one-word titles, such as 'Haunted' and 'Enough', to complete sentences ('She lacks confidence, she craves admiration insatiably. She lives on the reflections of herself in the eyes of others. She does not dare to be herself'). Key describes difficult characters with panache and apparent pleasure. Soulful and sunny, tight-laced and funny, Amy Key's poems illuminate their sad and sorry characters.

REFERENCES

Brahic, B.B. (2018) *The Hotel Eden.* Manchester: Carcanet Press.
Fan, K. (2018) *As Slow as Possible.* Todmorden: Arc Publications.
Key, A. (2018) *Isn't Forever.* Hexham: Bloodaxe Books.

Against Ageing

Vona Groarke, *Double Negative*
Deryn Rees-Jones, *Erato*

Double Negative by Vona Groarke (Carcanet, 2019) sounds like a book for our times, given the current political binaries. Seventeen titles of individual poems imply a fight against the negative: 'Against Anxiety', 'Against Despair', 'Against Boredom' etc. In a reading for Trinity College's English Department, Groarke admitted that, while teachers often tell poetry students to go easy on abstract nouns, she herself was drawn to the idea of using abstraction to make two words 'chafe against each other' and then 'agree in some odd or unforgettable fashion' (Groarke, 2018). 'Against Melancholy' has that odd quality (p.62):

> Let the evening shake itself dry like a dog
> so the tail is the last thing wriggiggling
> as, of course, you knew it would be.

The words 'melancholy' and 'wriggiggling' jar against each other. In case the leap from the abstract 'melancholy' to solid flesh in 'wriggiggling' does not convince, she reminds you that 'you' know the old phrase 'the tail wags the dog' so 'of course, you knew' that the tail would be the last thing moving. In this book, the very idea of the poem as a piece of writing is somehow negative, as in the ars poetica, 'This Poem' (p.18):

> This is the poem that cries on street corners
> and plays at being lost.
>
> This is the poem arranged at a tilt
> so all the words slide off.

Groarke's words do indeed slide off their most obvious meanings, and that has always been a delightful feature of her work because the slide is so finely judged. For example, in a prose poem, 'On Seeing Charlotte Brontë's Underwear with My Daughter in Haworth', the word 'year' has been forewarned as meaning season: 'With bad weather forecast and light silting up …The year settles in a corner …and set to one side its summer purse' (p. 40). The word 'year' segues into its academic sense in the next stanza, 'Half-term of her final year'. The poem is an elegy for the imminent loss of a daughter: 'We are buying time.' It is the last season of the year, the last year of the daughter's school or university course, and the last year that she will be living at home. Certain simple words, such as year, are repeated once from stanza to stanza or within stanzas, 'year… year', 'final…final', 'damson…damson', 'draws…draws', 'leaves…leave', the differences in meaning from line to line creating a delicate feel of slippage.

'Stone Trees' makes the reader aware of the fluctuating nature of words in a poem; their metaphorical richness glitters as 'amethyst, jasper, and chalcedony.' The speaker openly avows the poem's central lie, that her mother sewed: 'Here is her thread, her wherewithal, / filoselle from reeled silk, crewel yarn, cotton floss… My mother never sewed' (p.32). Always, Groarke demonstrates an awareness of sound: 'crewel yarn', if the reader listens carefully, surely suggests that the poem 'Stone Trees' is built around a fiction, since 'yarn' means fiction as well as thread. 'Aftermath Epigrams', the last poem in the collection, offers a far-ranging ars poetica (p.75). Groarke suggests here that a poem begins with no idea of its future development ('words blindfolded'), but it will need much cutting (words are 'made to walk the plank'). The poet will question the poem ('If it's a poem / it should have people in it. / I don't see anyone'), and her lines openly acknowledge their poetic nature, as in 'The Picture Window' (p.55):

> I wait as the keyhole waits
> for the ocean to get up from its white chair,
> shuck off these silky metaphors
> and, cursing my every idleness,
> take itself off down the shingle path
> that, obsequizing every step,
> has nothing, all the while, to say to me.

Perhaps this is an instance of the pathetic fallacy, with the ocean shucking off 'silky metaphors / and cursing my every idleness'. Surely not idle – there are prose poems here, epigraphs, a sonnet. Moreover, she mentions the word 'metaphor' often, possibly because an overarching metaphor in the collection is the one where words are life and life is telling her something important, as in 'Against Loneliness' (p.26):

The rain doesn't care so much for lists.
Tonight it calls by the house late
with something important to say.

Many of the 'double negative' poems have titles ending in double letters: loneliness, earnestness, loss. That final line can be read two ways: there is no room for anything between double letters or an absence (of youth, of pleasure) comes between them. Either the feeling of being alone is a kind of nothingness, concludes this study of loneliness, or nothing is a condition like 'empty-handed' rain. Groarke's poems explore behaviour with linguistic metaphors, and they examine their own method, though however overt Groarke's passion for language, this is no dry Oulipean application of rules. The overwhelming feeling this collection conveys is sadness, even though a characteristic Groarke position is defiance: 'which is fine by me', 'well, it's not as if I went looking for it', 'Who says?', 'What matter?'

Ageing is a major theme; winter has replaced summer: 'now is not August any more' ('Against Loneliness', p.26). Amid the book's awareness of ageing, the domestic minutiae in almost every poem, and the word play, the poems strive to avoid the simple binary of good v. bad. The first stanza of 'A to Z' explains that facts chafe against one another as do words (p.63):

Say one thing and straight away the opposite
hoves into view. That is why, perhaps, I am
indefinite – something to do with being Libran
or being short and therefore always riddled with
comparative fact.

Double Negative is the seventh collection of a poet whose later work increases rather than diminishes in intensity.

Much of the material in *Erato* (Seren, 2019), Deryn Rees-Jones's fifth collection, moves between elegy and ageing. As 'Firebird' asks, 'What stepping in / and back and on / is this, this middle age?' (p.46). The first poem in the book, for example, is a long prose poem, each section ending with an unspoken question: what do you make of that? ('Mon Amour', p.12).

The man who lived in the adjacent house in the terrace stopped me in the street one day and told me I was a disgrace to my profession. I was not even sure he knew what I did. Later he wrote me an unsigned letter, reinforcing my need for personal shame, insisting I cut down the tree in my backyard which towered across the rooftops.

The description conveys a powerlessness: the narrator is 'stopped… and told… I was not even sure…'. There is a sense of numbness that suits the material, alluding to Hiroshima as the title does. Rees-Jones counterpoints calm and agony, mature reflection and revulsion. 'Mon Amour' ends in a gothic manner, describing a wolf behind the bookcase, mentioning skin and bones, suggesting horror (p.14):

From the edges of my vision I was sure I saw a wolf slip with its yellow eyes from behind the bookcase to the room next door. I didn't want to check. The room was filled with a strange scent. Then the doorbell rang. The screen flickered. Skin. Bones. A doctor had said to me, We will watch, and wait.

Something I knew was only beginning.
Something, I knew, was at an end.

Rees-Jones's poems occasionally hinge in this way, with a prose account preceding a lyric statement. Here she chooses flora to open the lyric latch: 'The common laurel which I plan to fell / today can stand for love, this hell' ('I.M.', p.37). In 'Drone', though, politics ('I am listening to an interview with a man whose job it is to program / drones') leads to an account of lost sexual love (p.45):

We are lying naked in a small, badly lit room…
    I am moving a finger now down the line of hair which runs towards your groin… As I listen, the glass in the window shatters. In slow-motion you are reversed back into the evening, shaking time off your heels.

In this poem, Rees-Jones brilliantly enables the reader and narrator ('you' in the sense of anyone and/or the storyteller: 'In slow-motion you are reversed') to identify with the narrator's lover ('you' in the sense of a dying

partner: 'In a matter of seconds you have disappeared') (p.45). 'Fires'
also describes landscapes, personal and war-torn, ravaged by fire. It asks
(pp.41-2):

> What happens
>
> if we
>
> figure the lyric through this trauma, this movement in time
> between the workings of our unconscious/imagination, our con-
> nection with the moment of perception, being alive, and real?

'Fires' is a scholarly meditation (p.42):

> Like the after effects of trauma the fires keep returning,
> re-igniting. I chance upon a late, unfinished poem by Eliza-
> beth Bishop which recalls an incident in her infancy as she
> watched the nearby town of Salem being consumed by flames.
> 'A Drunkard' is a poem full of repetitions, verbal doublings –
>
> 'clearly clearly' 'reprimand reprimand'
>
> – a particular tic in Bishop's work, which appears to occur at
> moments when the 'nagging thoughts' that cannot quite be
> understood poke through.

The poem meditates on death and children, specifically the loss to her
children of their father, and it breaks up parental anxiety with analytic
rigour. Poems can have a transformative effect, turning the damage and
loss in life into organised lines. Rees-Jones has the analytic skill to explore
Bishop's poem and, in doing so, relive her own bereavement.

Erato is the Greek muse of lyric poetry, summoned in the book's
epigraph ('you goddess you – / guide your bard') to witness the poet's
own encounters with horror in the death of her lover and the father of
her children. Such a literary muse is a good model for a disquisition on
poetry, its erratic nature, its erasures and errors. '13 Numbered Fragments
Keeping Barbara Hardy in Mind' is a witty nod to Wallace Stevens's
'Thirteen Ways of Looking at a Blackbird' (Barbara Hardy is a literary
scholar). It mulls over the 'bad reader... the fearful reader, the reader in a

hurry to be determined' (p.65). We readers stand corrected. So do poets; the poem points to poetic practice as 'Failure in practice' and 'Getting things wrong' (p.65). Here, mis-takes are the creative achievement, the poem that flies round the scholastic library and sings ('Nightjar', p.67):

> Listen to the nightjar, hear her holy tremblings –
> star litter, night fragment, slip down a spine of grass.

References

Groarke, V. (2019) *Double Negative*. Manchester: Carcanet Press.

The University of Dublin, Trinity College (2018) *Vona Groarke Reading at Trinity College*. Available at: https://youtu.be/dU85-L3VwU4?feature=shared (accessed: 29 January 2024).

Rees-Jones, D. (2019) *Erato*. Bridgend: Seren.

Poetry of Dualities

Tishani Doshi, *A God at the Door*
Alice Hiller, *bird of winter*
Christopher Meredith, *Still*

The title of Tishani Doshi's fourth collection, *A God at the Door*, reads like a threat. Hear that knock? You'd better open up because it's a god. Eighty-nine pages of long and long-lined poems call on readers to listen to their angry and anxious reactions to contemporary horrors: Covid-19, migration, disaster, war, rape. Sometimes the tone is sarcastic, as in this passage from 'End-of-Year Epiphany at the Holiday Inn' (p.102):

> So what if a man is slaughtered and set alight
> for love, for a slab of dead cow, for reasons
> sacred? So what if the waters are rising
> and those seas will soon be upon us?
> We must live in the moments we're given.

The poet uses 'we' and 'you' frequently in the book to address the reader, inviting, cajoling, insisting: 'can't we?', 'let us', 'you could be', 'we must'. 'We' could be you the reader and I the speaker, us human beings, or simply the plural subject of an individual poem; it is often a representative of 'our people' as in 'Creation Abecedarian' (p.13). In 'Mandala', the first poem, Doshi describes the thrill and threat of being socially constructed selves (p.11):

> We stitch our days and nights, one to the other,
>   and it's like embroidering a galaxy, but even galaxies
> recede from one another...
>   Sometimes we leave
> the house without our masks and it's a relief to take a break
>   from who we are...

'Who we are' is also the 'we' who have left the house, and the reader senses that the masks taken off on the doorstep are replaced in the street with other masks. Later in the collection, drawing on the reader's identification with the poem's narrator, Doshi tells 'us' that 'we' are contradictory beings (p.101):

> We are homesick everywhere
> even when we're home   we are empty things
> that need filling
> we are always lost in love   never found
> please come find me.

These lines, like so many in this collection, spill out like confessions, drawing the reader inside the narrator's unease with striking observations, as in 'Tigress Hugs Manchurian Fur' (p.50):

> The forest is
> awash in a dial of light more
> luminiferous than a Canaletto. I
> misuse the words forest, woodland,
> jungle because I have never walked
> alone through forest, woodland, jungle.
> I say Canaletto because I long to be in a
> place of light different from this place of light.

Note the display of narrator self-awareness: Doshi uses the physics term 'luminiferous' and immediately acknowledges that 'I / misuse …words'. Misuse is, perhaps, Doshi's major theme. Politicians, punters and gods all misuse our world, while the reader is given tongue-in-cheek reassurance (p.77):

> Do not worry. This is war, where the women,
> like metaphors, are always steadfast and beautiful.
> In history's version she sits under the peepal tree
> with your Victoria Cross pinned to her sari.

Even her irony, as shown here, is an exemplar of misuse: the lines suggest the writer is a disenchanted citizen, making a personification of 'history' who will give 'versions' rather than facts. The role of the poet, this collection suggests, is to pull dualities such as light/dark, pain/joy, and we/them into measured shape, and the impressive shaping of many of the poems on the page echoes this process. It's a hectoring read, politically

and poetically relevant to a world that wants a prophet and finds only
false ones.

Alice Hiller's first collection, *bird of winter,* concerns childhood
sexual abuse, 'working with her childhood and adolescent medical notes'
to depict 'a crime to which millions around the world are subjected', as
the back cover states. The book is an impressive example of the power of
poetic control, in its choice of what information to share with the reader
and in its simplicity of diction and varied use of line.

The absence of guiding punctuation (apart from the quotation marks
in erasure poems) is telling. There are no stops here, not even commas to
barrack words, but also no calling out with capitals, no screaming with
exclamation marks. The first poem, 'o dog of pompeii', suggests why: 'I
want to release that studded collar / chained hound of my underworld'
(p.1). The poems throw off the tethers of socially sanctioned silences
around abuse till the unpunctuated and carefully punctured lines soar
(p.1):

> ... I lost you   beloved playmate
> as a finger   moved inward
>
> forcing me   whimpering
> down warrens   of dark tunnels

The gaps in the lines form a vagina-like fissure that, in the context of
phrases such as 'as a finger   moved inward', is painful to see. There are
no guards, such as full stops and commas would give. Hiller's timing of
disclosure is rigorous in 'elegy for an eight year old' (p.49):

> mr ward says she's moving
> onto the green book for maths
>
> underneath her wool tights
> the hurt place stays on fire

In addition to Hiller's omitting punctuation, many other techniques
illuminate the theme, including erasure ('the House of the Faun'), the
blank black untitled page, and concrete poems, such as 'sagittae', a picture
of three arrows each composed with the same words. The relentless image,
that repeats three times, appears to the reader as both warlike and phallic.

Hiller suggests disaster by other means too, for example creating a backdrop of Pompeii and Herculaneum: poems may have a note floating in space nearby describing a part of those lost cities or might use a relevant text. For example, the poem 'let none of this enter you' has these lines, 'I would rather the masts / of your boats put out my eyes', which lie above and to one side of a lineated quote from Pliny the Younger's letter describing the eruption at Pompeii: 'and now the ashes were falling / on the ships thicker and hotter / the closer they approached and / also pumice stones and cinders' (p.24). '[P]umice stones' are not only part of the volcanic eruption of Pompeii, but are also used by bathers to scrub away dirt, and the phrase echoes the 'bath / where she has peed already', lines in the poem above the quote. It is as if history has previously acted out our nightmares, that the horrors we endure are written in the landscape of our past.

At the end of 'o dog of pompeii', a small prose poem floats centrally on its own page, suggesting the powerlessness of guards against catastrophe. This brings the reader out of the poem's four nightmare sections, where the guard dog, buried under 'metres of ash and pumice', cannot function to guard the house's inhabitants. The final section uses public language to describe art: mosaics, it announces, show houseguests one reality (that the house is a protected space) while the detached tone of the prose poem, like any label in a museum or historic space, allows irony to emerge: here is art showing what, in reality, did not happen. Home is a protected space only if a child is safe from abuse.

Hiller balances fact with commentary in 'the needle's eye sews red silk' (p.4):

pain distils its own weather

repeated rape of same victim by single offender
15 years custody

sometimes death extends a hand

Through this poem, the offence and its punishment escalate, from a single offence of rape of a child (ten years old) to sustained attack. At that point death could have intervened: 'sometimes death extends a hand'. The poem balances these legalised definitions against lyrical lines that, though brief, summon up the massive pain of rape, such as 'harsh as ash over sunshine' (p.4). As well as the Pompeiian tragedy, the phrase alludes to the aftermath of Hiroshima, that bombing of the innocent by a major power. Rape is not a once-and-forgotten act; it causes long-term suffering to its victim.

A text written by 'scipio maffei on the excavations at herculaneum November 1747' appears as a prose poem. This use of quotation as poetry, the collaging of texts with lyric, is a modernist technique here used for the arduous task of gathering and sharing information about abuse. Such a task is more usually and importantly the province of courts and communities. How difficult it must be to encourage a child to speak; how painful it is for an abused individual to expose their suffering. With their gaze resolutely on the grievous effects arising from abuse, these poems reproach the act of looking away. *bird of winter* will turn your gaze towards damaging behaviours that we know happen but can't bear to focus on. The whole work is an elegy for a childhood.

Still, Christopher Meredith's sixth collection, establishes a pause for thought – which is what a poem can be, a needful rest, a meditation. The word 'still' recurs in many of these poems, functioning as an active verb, an adjective, an adverb, or a preposition; these poems encourage you to stop for a second to allow the depth of their meaning to emerge. The title poem uses 'still' to suggest *stationary* as well as *ongoing* and, cleverly, as *a producer of alcohol* in 'Still' (p.8):

Memory is the still of slow forgetting,
the black and aching decades boiled to air,

cooled to this crawling droplet in the pipe
moving still and still in this suspension
rolling on its empty convolutions
to catch and lose a world in hard white light.

This discourse on what is kept and what is lost through one's life is rhythmically calm. Another meaning of still, a photographic still, also appears in several poems. 'Air Cameras' describes memories of a past happy occasion when taking photographs, without using the word 'still.' Photographic plates feature in 'Stereoscope,' etchings in 'John Blight at the Lands End' (p.14):

and I stood where the rock shore stands
and falls away
essayed in the same scratched plate
to remake its granite stacks and blocks
and render the unthinking tide
to move and still atlantics
in the one carved line…

Photography can 'still atlantics' as memory can do and as some poetry aims to do in such evocative lines as these, giving us the idea, the sensation even, of life in any of its forms, of wild Atlantics on a page. Other arts perform the work of bringing people to a kind of stillness, such as music. 'Solstice' suggests music by means of describing 'the woods in snow' (p.66):

> bird minims climb
>> the invisible stair
> that winds in the
> ghostpale winter air
>
> and under the whitening
>> darkening hill
> music paces
>> paces
>>> still.

The 'woods in snow' seem both static and melodic: the positioning of lines and even of letters within words exemplifies this dualism. Overall, the tone of the collection is predictably quiet.

Yet the last poem, 'Winter Woods', rages like a storm. Meredith begins with a quasi-lecture on how snow is formed or 'conjured,' and there's nothing still about this process: 'specks of earth… whirl,' snowflakes 'rock and float, slide, sideslip, / tumble, float again / ride down the zigzag / seesaws of the half-sustaining air' (p.68). In the last stanza, after snow falls on his face, the narrator suddenly breaks his book-long calm and cries out: 'Was there ever a lousier metaphor / for death?' You could say all metaphors fall apart in the way snow dissolves: think it through, and disassociation follows. Yes, death is as still and quiet as snow is once it settles. After sixteen published works of fiction and poetry, *Still* shows

Meredith isn't ready to settle yet, and he calls triumphantly to the reader in the final line: 'The cold catch in the throat says we're alive' (p.69). His creativity refuses to be still.

REFERENCES

Doshi, T. (2021) *A God at the Door*. Hexham: Bloodaxe Books.
Hiller, A. (2021) *bird of winter*. Liverpool: Pavilion Poetry, Liverpool University Press.
Meredith, C. (2021) *Still*. Bridgend: Seren.

Veronica Forrest-Thomson, Modernism, and Me

I came to writing poetry in the late 1990s after many years as a consumer magazine journalist, and, as such, I knew what was important: the reader, the British consumer-reader. I knew they wanted a storyline, and I could provide that. In fact, since journalists put their most important facts up front, I gave them stories they could repeat to friends without even reading the whole piece.

Originally, I thought a poetry reader would be like those magazine readers, hungry for summaries. Indeed, bestselling poetry collections of the nineties seem to me to foreground a simple extractable storyline. But I had a problem: the words, the syntax, and all the other grammatical paraphernalia that I had smoothed down and pushed out of sight in the onward rush of a magazine feature became more important and more noticeable in my poems. For example, lines broke in syntactically unusual places, and these breakages complicated the simple extractable storyline I had aimed for. Poems resisted my journalistic narrative habits.

During the process of transitioning from writing consumer journalism to writing poetry, I cast around for theorists in order to understand the different styles of poetry, and came across Veronica Forrest-Thomson's poetics. She wrote: 'To take a language and organise it in rhymed stanzas, making use of a rhetorical tone and figurative combinations or words, is a social act which emphasises formal features normally irrelevant to the business of communication' (2016, p.107). Reading that, I felt much better, since I had felt that form should dominate, or at least direct, meaning in a poem. Poetry is all about form, I wanted to believe, and a poem is form. I didn't want a reader to take a meaning, a narrative, or story out of a poem. As Archibald MacLeish says in his well-known poem, 'Ars Poetica': 'A poem should not mean but be' (n.d.). This line is part of the title of 'Cordelia', one of Veronica Forrest-Thomson's poems, and it declares that the poem itself is the story (2008, p.152). As she wrote, 'The world comes to us through words and may very well be created by them....' (2016, p.113). If words create the world, then they create the poem's narrative too.

I started to think of Forrest-Thomson as my grandmother poet, a poet who goes before you and shows you the way, which is ironic as she was born in the same year that I was, in 1947, in Malaysia. She left Malaysia aged three and grew up in Scotland. She became an academic, gaining a first-class English degree from Liverpool University, then a PhD from Cambridge (where one of her supervisors was the modernist poet, J.H. Prynne), pursued postdoctoral research at Leicester and began work as a lecturer at Birmingham. In 1975, aged 27, Veronica Forrest-Thomson died, a sudden and tragic event, involving an overdose thought to be accidental. Despite the very young age at which she died, she had written major works of literature, both critical and creative.

Importantly, she had written a theoretical work, *Poetic Artifice*, published by Manchester University Press three years after her death. This book is where I first found her ideas. A newer edition, edited by Gareth Farmer, was published by Shearsman Books in 2016. *Poetic Artifice*, a complex and exciting read, supported my poetic practice. Much of its thinking has influenced me, perhaps most profoundly her ideas on complexity. A poetic narrative, she suggests, doesn't have to be simple. A poem can overtly present a sense of complexity both linguistic and syntactical. For a modernist poet like Forrest-Thomson, a poem is an openly complicated thing – intertextual, fragmented. Less obvious is her notion that the poem should acknowledge its complexity, as though the very being of a poem must be made obvious to the reader.

There's a key phrase in *Poetic Artifice* acknowledging poetic complexity: *image-complex*. Forrest-Thomson wasn't the first critic to use the term. Ezra Pound, a poet who interested her, said famously, 'An image is an intellectual and emotional complex in an instant of time.' (Pound, n.d.). Forrest-Thomson defines an image-complex as 'where we can discover the thematic, semantic, rhythmical and formal patterns that are important to a poem' (2016, p.47).

The image-complex appeared to me to provide an alternative to the summarisable meaning that many readers want from a poem. Forrest-Thomson believed that the reader was important – she understood post-structuralism, which suggests that the reader has a vital role in the construction of a poem's meanings – but, she wrote, the reader must not be seduced by the conventional idea that poems should make sense according to the external world. She called this idea '*bad naturalisation*' (2016, pp.223-226). Other contemporary poets have picked up on this point. Keston Sutherland said in 2008, quoting *Poetic Artifice*, that a reader 'should not objectionably turn poems into stories about life, history, and the world' (Sutherland, n.d.). Such stories, this suggests, were what readers of such poets as Philip Larkin and other so-called Movement poets were given. Sandeep Parmar (2015) writes,

'As I read postwar British poetry fully, I became less enamoured with the Movement tones of Philip Larkin or Donald Davie and reviled their small, digestible, miserable artefacts of everyday British life, what Andrew Duncan likens to the 1950s domestic white goods of an individualist capitalist economy.'

Larkin's poems, for example, offer a simple expression of feeling, despair, anger, wryness, with an explanatory story attached. Frequently, his final stanza jumps from a well-grounded narrative to a different and broad perspective, as if the ending could supply a grander vision.

I decided that I would not write poems about life, but aim at image-complexes, whatever that might mean for my own poetry. Again, Forrest-Thomson gave me plenty of poems for models. She was a practitioner as well as a theorist, having written five collections of poetry by the age of 27, and she enacted her ideas in her own poetry. While her ideas gave me permission to experiment, her poems gave me energy: they are fresh, funny, intellectual, parodic, and distinctively her own. For example, 'Zettel', a poem that refers to one of Wittgenstein's publications, deals distinctively with the interplay of form, language, and meaning (2008, p.77):

With the configuration of chess-pieces
limbs describe themselves in rooms
under the angle-poise.
"What is the opposite of brown?
– orange?
– another shade
of brown."
Limbs of the angle alter,
poise, in rooms:
what is the opposite of me?
– you?
– another shade
of me.

The lamp is connected to human limbs: the word 'limbs' occurs in lines nearby, and the words 'angle' and 'poise' are broken and rearranged. Subsequent words cross enjambments, like the elbow of an Anglepoise lamp. Repeating words are 'poised' above each other, answers are 'poised' below questions, grammatical constructions (i.e. if…then) are poised in lines. And the poem looks at different 'angles' of meaning.

With all the language play, I read 'Zettel' as a deconstructed romantic love poem (2008, p.77):

> Roomspace in which we dispose
> ourselves is not external.
> The gap between
> my purple trousers
> and his pale-green shirt
> is then
> grammatical.
> I love you.
> One says the ordinary thing
> – with the wrong gesture.

What love is, in this particular case, or who is speaking, or how many, if any, particular persons, doesn't matter. Love as a feeling is broken and reconstructed in language. The poem continues: 'Love is not a feeling. / Love is put to the test / – the *grammatical* test'. The obsession with 'I', notably in Romantic poetry, becomes poignantly 'the first person singular', for what do you feel when you are most in love but your singularity and the absence of your lover? You feel the impossibility of getting the beloved close enough, even if they are holding you in the curve of their elbow like an Anglepoise lamp, when they are close enough to shed light on your life.

'Zettel', a romantic, linguistically aware poem, suggests why critics debate whether Forrest-Thomson's poems are modernist, late modernist, postmodern or post-structuralist. Her poetry references Derrida, Kristeva, Empson, Pound, Plato, and Dr Johnson. 'Zettel' finishes with these lines (2008, pp.78-9):

> The concept of a living being
> has the same indeterminacy
> as that of a language.
>
> […]

The *same* indeterminacy though,
which could suggest a cast-
list drawn up in language
play, that speech commits
to fantasy. And so it does
at least in the first
person singular, for:
One's hand writes
it does not write because one wills
but one wills
what it writes.

This meditation on the human being as an idea, a 'concept', being uncertain, appeals to me; I experience other human beings in daily life as badly drawn, dimly recognisable, unclear. That draws me to write poetry, as a 'language play' that will 'cast' others to see how they then appear. Such attempts are not easy. Forrest-Thomson's collection *Language-Games* tackles the difficulty of writing, as she explains in the preface. The poems were written out of her admiration and understanding of Wittgenstein; in his treatise *Zettel*, he wrote: 'Do not forget that a poem, even though it is composed in the language of information, is not used in the language-game of giving information' (Perloff, p.185). Certainly, Forrest-Thomson's 'Zettel' exemplifies what it calls the 'indeterminacy of language'; this is not information but indication. The poem suggests that the mind goes where it will and that it might interpret what the brain receives in many different ways: 'a cast- / list drawn up in language / play, that speech commits / to fantasy' (p.79).

I wrote my fourth collection, *Solar Cruise*, several years after first reading Forrest-Thomson's work, and I wanted the book to be about how to think about what you do, about whose thinking you want to know and reference, about how to think together – with the reader, with the poem's characters. The two characters in *Solar Cruise* are partners – a poet and a physicist – who tackle climate change in their different ways and take a journey toward an improved climate. It's a loose, fragmentary narrative, and it includes data relating to the physics of solar energy. Including science, data as well as theory, was challenging and not something I had done very often in precious collections. So I was interested that, in 1971, Forrest-Thomson wrote her PhD for Cambridge University on *Poetry as Knowledge: The Use of Science by Twentieth-Century Poets*. She says in 'Impersonal Statement': 'If there must be a justification for making poems it is surely that they provide the same kind of data concerning the inter-actions of man and his environmental situations as does science only in different terms' (p.164). Similarly, I wanted the language of science to inform the language of love in *Solar Cruise*. The book relates to my partner's work: in the fight to find safer forms of energy, he uncovered a new area of physics – the quantum well solar cell. Physics is a language describing nature's artifice, and a physicist's life is one of discovering structures: I found these congenial subjects for a collection of poems.

To make my own contribution to the fight for safer energy, I wanted to construct a poetics of love – love of the earth as much as of a lover. Again, Forrest-Thomson was helpful. She wrote, in the preface to her collection *On the Periphery*, that knowledge is reconciled to love through style: 'Indeed such equation of love with knowledge and the idea of style as their reconciliation is as old as the art itself, for the other person is the personification of the other, the unknown, the external world and all one's craft is necessary to catch him' (2008, p.168). The idea that my partner personified the external world appealed to me, and Forrest-Thomson's suggestion that verbal craft can offer versions of reality that enhance understanding of 'the other', those we do not immediately understand, strengthened my concept of *Solar Cruise*. The book is a long love poem, human love and climate care fused by what I found to be the most useful style, a collocation of short narratives, data excerpted from scientific reports and papers, and lyric musings. The ordering of these fragments is key to indicate their importance and relevance to each other as much as they inform and relieve the reader's hard work, in turn. I included a picture of Keith's hand with his invention, the solar cell, on his palm to illustrate the human being behind the physics. Further, I describe his everyday working habits, give a picture of the room, the desk we both use, and infuse those visual details with my own thoughts and questions that I have directed to him throughout our working partnership. I have described how we work together on interconnected projects, as well as our varying professional practices in physics and poetry: thus, climate change becomes operational; some people can tackle it by doing their job. Moreover, avoiding climate change is a communal activity, and part of my job as a contributor to avoiding climate change is to support the climate workers' network to which my partner belongs.

Both physics and poetry involve constant questioning. Is *Solar Cruise* lyric? Is it modernist? The book poses numerous questions, as in this passage, from 'Are We Wasting Our Time?' (p.32):

> Our rocking sea
> is floor and ground and base and shoe, and I
> am not sure
> footed on it. I might not get over
> to our future though I row, row, row, row, row
> in my head, in my middle ear that lies
> between one hair and another, sickening,
> constantly whispering,
>
> > *the voyage*
> > *is wrong and you are wrong and he is wrong*
> > *and sea is not stability.*
>
> Sea's built right,
> but I am not a rower and I would not.

Perhaps the major impact Forrest-Thomson has had on my work, through her theory and her poems, is to have established for me the fact that poetry, even lyric love poetry, is 'resolutely artificial', and it is okay if it sounds artificial. Nor does it have to present polemic, as prose might do, or deliver a logical or coherent narrative, in order to contribute to, to change even, the future of human life.

References

Crowther, C. (2020) *Solar Cruise: A Memoir.* Bristol: Shearsman Books.

Forrest-Thomson, V. (1971) *Poetry as Knowledge: The Use of Science by Twentieth-Century Poets.* PhD Thesis. University of Cambridge.

Forrest-Thomson, V. (2008) *Collected Poems.* Edited by A. Barnett. Exeter: Shearsman Books.

Forrest-Thomson, V. (2016) *Poetic Artifice: A Theory of Twentieth-Century Poetry.* Edited by G. Farmer. Bristol: Shearsman Books.

MacLeish, A. (n.d.) *Ars Poetica.* Available at: https://poets.org/poem/ars-poetica (accessed: 8 February 2024).

Parmar, S. (2015) 'Not a British Subject: Race and Poetry in the UK', December 6, *Los Angeles Review of Books.* Available at: https://lareviewofbooks.org/article/not-a-british-subject-race-and-poetry-in-the-uk (Accessed: 8 February 2024).

Perloff, M. (1996) *Wittgenstein's Ladder*. Chicago: The University of Chicago Press.

Pound, E. (no date) *A Few Don'ts by an Imagiste*. Available at: https://www.poetryfoundation.org/poetrymagazine/articles/58900/a-few-donts-by-an-imagiste (accessed: 8 February 2024).

Sutherland, K. (n.d.) 'Veronica Forrest-Thomson for Readers'. Available at: https://kenyonreview.org/kr-online-issue/index-2/selections/ (accessed: 8 February 2024).

Wittgenstein, L. (2001) *Tractatus Logico-Philosophicus*. Translated by D.F. Pears and B.F. McGuinness. London: Routledge.

Wittgenstein, L. (1967) *Zettel*. Translated by G.E.M. Anscombe and G.H. von Wright. Oxford: Blackwell.

II.

Interviews

Stretch of Closures
(Shearsman, 2007)

CE: Tell me about putting together your first collection *Stretch of Closures,* and your poetics at this stage.

CC: It was a time of intensity and exhilaration. Firstly, I wanted a page, and I wanted words – just those two things. I am a page poet in the most traditional sense (though I did once write a poem to be placed on a window and, when I look at that window poem placed on a page, the four lines of it sit unhappily cramped and shivering at the top of a white mountain). I had been a journalist, and I loved getting thoughts and data into threads of whatever discourse might be needed. But as a journalist, always working to a set number of words, I had been longing for mastery of and freedom on the physical page. I thought the page could be a physical holding of what I carried, what we all carry, from years of looking and thinking and feeling. I was fifty years old when I started to write poetry; *Stretch of Closures* is what I (eventually) wrote. I could move on the page beyond prose, but still have bits of prose if I wanted. I could let lines build along with their meanings. I could stop and start in stanzas of various shapes and sizes. I thought and still think poetry needs mess, controlled mess, as life does.

Secondly, I had just completed an MPhil at the University of South Wales; Matthew Francis was my mentor, and he was exemplary. I lived in Italy and the USA during the first year of the MPhil and discovered North American poetry down in the basement stacks of the University of California, Berkeley library. Lorine Niedecker's work handed me everything I needed to know about how facts and words coalesce into a poem on the page. I went to a reading at City Lights bookstore in San Francisco (or it might have been an adjacent bar) and heard Thom Gunn read; he was my introduction to syllabic poetry. Writing *Stretch of Closures* was like stepping into a newly cracked-open geode.

CE: What do you think you've drawn from your reading of Niedecker? Could you say a bit more about what she showed you in terms of data, words, and the page?

Niedecker is an exemplar of absence, space and brake. Though I didn't tend to emulate her absence of punctuation and of title, I learned from reading her poetry how to make every word work hard in a line, how weightless words can be as well as weighty, how you can make them float or anchor them where they need to be on the page. You can also suggest words you don't use, a tactic I admire. Paul Muldoon mentions this in his Oxford lectures. You can see it clearly in Niedecker's poem 'Paul', where the word 'leaves' hums with the word 'lives' and 'lie' suggests 'die'. Niedecker also showed me how to express anger through minimal information, as in her poem 'Fall' in *The Granite Pail* (p.243):

> High class human
> got no illumine
>
> how a ten cent plant
> winds aslant
>
> around a post.

The tone here is unmistakably derisory. The adjectival phrase 'high class' on the first line presents a person of supposedly superior social status, while the second line undercuts that with a hard and ungrammatical verb – 'got'. 'Got' suggests a lower status that does, whatever social norms might suggest about superior and inferior classes, have 'illumine'. The frustration and anger vented in this inversion – high class being low insight, low class being high wisdom – is clear from this short stanza alone.

Some of what impresses me about Niedecker arises from her being influenced by Objectivism in early twentieth-century North American poetry. That interaction resulted in what she called her 'condensery', stacking up words and images, blow by blow, lightning dashes between heart and head in such brilliant poems as 'Paean to Place' (Niedecker, p.14).

I felt admiration for the disciplined way Niedecker allowed into her poetry a difficult personal life spent mostly in isolation on the banks of Black Hawk Island (in a cottage I've visited): she seems to have been irritatingly, appealingly, self-effacing in her life as a poet. I had not read any poet's work as striking as hers at that stage of my writing.

CE: As I read *Stretch of Closures,* the opening poems become very gradually more elliptical, steadily leaving larger gaps in the discourse of a poem. How did you conceive of this ellipticism for yourself?

CC: I think ellipticism is a poetry of absence, as I've noted in Niedecker's work. There is a mass withdrawal of words and lines that happens when the poem I am contemplating applies itself to a page; the poem covers the resulting holes, as a memory makes a coherent picture which is not the same as a photograph. In fact, the memory creates a picture, which might be very different from reality. If I do this process well, it results in an extreme economy. If I write poorly, the poem is needlessly obscure. I go to great lengths not to be obscure.

    This is to say ellipticism is the result of my overall process, which has been the same throughout my years of writing poetry. I start with an outgush of words, no lines, no shapes. I file it away. I take it out later, read it aloud, and remove some words knowing, for that one edit, exactly what needs removing. I file it away. I repeat for a year or so. Lineation, of course, is another way to cut. At last I have something that needs only a bit extra (another space, another word, another line, another stanza) to function. I put in that bit extra. Not much extra. Absence remains. When readers find my poems elliptical, I hope they take that as part of the experience of the poem, because this is a poetic that invites the reader to engage with their own response. I have never wanted to tell the reader anything – just to point with a few words.

CE: The third poem, 'Wouldn't Couldn't Weren't' (p.15), ends each line with a contracted verb, creating a kind of optical end rhyme. Do you see this poem as a kind of invented form or playing against a given restriction? How do you use form or self-imposed restriction in your creative process?

CC: Form, whatever it might be in any particular poem, is hugely important. There is a point in the poem's development, and it doesn't come straight away to me, when both the form, the way the words appear on the page, and the single words and phrases themselves with their multiple meanings and feelings start to join up. This poem portrays the relationship between a recalcitrant child and her mother, between a recalcitrant family and a neighbour, between a recalcitrant language and a settled line with expectations and frustrations. Lines are always being stopped in this poem by the very word 'not' in its half-absent form 'n't'. The interior of the poem is ringing with words of restriction: 'stay', 'reversing', 'catch', 'squeezer', 'hold'. There is a word inherent but not voiced in the poem, 'risk', which must be evaluated by the actors in the poem and then acted on. A child might die; a mother might be condemned by uptight neighbours; an uptight neighbour might release a long-pent breath. Risk begins and ends with restriction and loosens restriction. Poems call for restriction as a formal mode of being. Form today is the opposite of arrest: it is diverse; it can develop during a poem, even resulting in a significant difference between the appearance of the beginning and end of a poem.

I was lucky to start writing at the end of the twentieth century, a time when British poetry had developed a sort of corset of Larkinism: easy idiomatic vocabulary, a narrative, a strong 'I' voice to a poem, and an emotional epiphany at the end. This is a generalisation, but I felt there were different ways to write a poem, and I wasn't particularly concerned with identifying myself with any one school. I dipped into a melee of styles, British, European, North American, and read enough to be aware I had numerous choices available while drafting a poem. Form grows with a poem. They become the same thing. Form is the recognisable face and personality of a poem.

CE: On rereading the book, I was amused by the latter section titles, 'Untitled' for the third section and 'Forthcoming Titles' for the fourth. Are these titles intended as a gesture against closure in the manuscript, or did you have another intention?

CC: I hate titles. Well, they are useful, but perhaps are best kept simple for new poets. I was acknowledging that this is a first collection: simple groupings of my best poems so far and a sign of things to come, hopefully. There was a rationale to the section titles, allied loosely to life stages: child, adult, old age, after death. Closure is important to the book, hence the overall title. Of course, sending a poem off into a book is a closure, after months or years of work on it.

CE: One of the book's most pervasive themes is the maternal, and sometimes its presence is startling, as in 'Caught by Workmen', which opens 'Sometimes, like a mother, / a blackened burned building // collapses' (p.40). Could you say something about the importance of the maternal to this collection?

CC: The language of birth seeps into these poems all over the place, even at the end. The penultimate poem, about the end of learning (it never ends so that notion is a kind of death) mentions 'midwifery' and 'delivery', and the language in its middle section resembles the encouragement you'll hear from your midwife when you give birth. This emphasis wasn't deliberate. Giving birth is a surreal experience, and writing poetry calls on every surreal experience you have had. Also, I do feel maternal about a poem. It is born, in a mess, covered in blood, and you clean it and feed it and it takes ages to grow and you feel you are ageing because of it. You also have a huge responsibility to it. Of course, the metaphorical resonance of the whole book, which is the birth into the world of these poems, will be gestatory.

It took a bookful of poems to move out of the primigravida-poet stage. After the first book is out, you have a more mature attitude to yourself as a poet. Not least because you can at last say 'Yes' when people ask, as they always do when they come across a single poem, 'Have you published a book?' A book is not a chance thing. After producing one, I began expecting every new poem I wrote to operate both on its own and as a member of my family of books, because now I knew there was one. That enlarged my vision and made me look at a poem as a waystation to a larger body of work, which would have its own overall expression of something different in each single poem.

CE: Another of the book's prominent themes is language and its uses. I think of the end of 'Caught by Workmen' (p.40) where the traffic 'laughs / in another language' and 'Ticket Language' (p.20) with the language of British public transport. Was this kind of metapoetic consideration of language part of the gestatory process you talked about – a kind of working out of your relationship to language in the process of writing the poems?

CC: Yes, indeed. Firstly, I am delighted to be working with words, I know they are words, the reader knows it. I'm affecting the reader with words as they affect me. I don't want to write the sort of poem that has been very popular in the English-speaking world till recently, the narrative that ends with an epiphany. I want to play, and here are the devices of the game: words, lines, space, and page.

But it's a serious game off-page, so, while I'm in the world of printed words, I can point out how other people are playing with words, in ways that have an effect on us; I can make some social observations that way. For example, I don't know what language my or any children are using, and trying to talk to them will result in the upset of my norms. The daughter I mention in the first poem of the collection, 'Reconstructive Fortressing' (p.13), is also the reader/listener. I am always maternal about a listener, not protective but wanting the best. But the daughter/reader/ listener 'is going to have to give up her view', meaning develop another or wider perspective on life. And so am I. I had decided that writing poems from the position of enquiry rather than supposition, asking questions rather than trying to promote an already decided viewpoint, is the only useful approach. That means language must be open and expansive, and sometimes I have to make it up. Towards the end of 'Stretch of Closures', I describe the renewing of a verge: 'Covered in soot, the men bite away / old markings ready for a new language' (p.92). There are many boundaries in the book, and many of them refer to the need for a new response, language being mine. 'Cheval de Frise' (p.70) is a wall with broken glass on top, so I ask the reader: 'What blank thing / do you look at without altering?' 'The Sentence Mender' describes this process: 'I carry my voice out at night away from, our house to West Hill junction [...] then I storm this firmament, / blare from scaffolding, against murders of windows, in the drizzle of twenty-four-hour supermarkets' (p.54). And hearing is vital to a poem: 'My ear is like a shell the wind swept' ('Lost Child', p.28). The sound of the poem, of its phrasing and overall rhythms, is essential to any poem's meanings.

To address your question more precisely: yes, I tried and still do try not to impose a particular language on a new poem, but discover one for the poem, an accent you could call it, during my lengthy writing process. I tend to start out with Anglo-Saxonish, short words, very few Latinate or long words. Then over time, as I discover the meaning of a poem, I will have to refine its language, its sound, its linguistic reverberations. In 'Flag Waver', there is a bed of short Middle-English-derived words (I believe): 'His car dips, almost kneels / perhaps to the black cave' (p.53). This bed will be part of the early version of the poem. I have a family feel for this sort of language, as I suggest in 'Marriage, Off Season': 'A turn to a dry hamlet through fields / as homely as Warwickshire' (p.52). Warwickshire, where I grew up, is the home of William Shakespeare, and I am deeply familiar with its ancient phrases. My Birmingham-born father, however, used short words. As I go on, I add in or replace words with language that reflects the character of the particular poem. This can be less plain, with more complications of syllables and longer sentences, as in 'Against the Evidence' (p.47), a poem that begins in England and goes, by train, to Italy, where the language melts and mixes:

> When soft Lecce stone is cut
> the guide says, in loro posso virtute,
> che le pregia, e che l'indura:
> virtue enriches it and hardens it.

CE: I find your use of hybrid poems, bringing together both prose and lines, particularly appealing in how you move between the fluent unspooling of prose and the definite white space at the end of the line in such works as 'Spin', 'The Sentence Mender' and 'Weekend in Belgium'. Did you have any particular inspiration for this combination of prose and lines, and how do you view it?

CC: I have no poets to mention particularly in this regard, though many poets use this device, and I must have read some while writing this collection. Nor am I conscious of reading *haibuns* at that time; I have since. The reason those hybrid poems are there is for just the reasons outlined earlier: a poem sometimes develops a prose voice, maybe another register, and then lineation doesn't work. I put those lines into prose, and the poem relaxes again. But that poem may still need its other register, its other voice, a lineated voice, and I then include a lineated section. There are always many voices speaking just outside the poem, their words don't appear in the open, but somehow the poem's words raise those other words – this is simply because every word has its associations – these outsider voices are more like murmurs than voices, suggesting rhyming couplets, maybe, or exploded stanzas or any sort of form; I listen, but try not to let them disturb the maturing poem. Allowing prose and lines to work together is only one of many mixed form choices for a poem.

The space adjustments were particularly difficult to work through on those poems. I should say here that I still have some difficulty with the varying of the last word in a prose line; a prose poem has a variable last word, depending on font, size and type, and size of page. So the words turn simply where space and font size make them turn and, in any prose poem, there could be different line endings in different publications. I had to allow the sentence to tower over this non-lineated passage, or set of lines as I see it, in a way that it doesn't, I feel, when the last word in a line is fixed. In later books, I experimented with moving the prose to the right of the page. This helped me look ever more closely at the effect of the small word, the preposition, the pronoun, the connective when it falls at the end of a line in a non-lineated piece. And I increased that attention in lineated poems as well.

I feel this loosening of lineation, while giving covert attention to it, makes 'The Sentence Mender' one of the more successful poems in the collection. The material is angry and vocal, and the form is also cross and disjointed. The final two lines suggest dysfunction in the language: 'I work on it in the garage / a sentence mender' (p.54). From the first section, I try to give a sense of more than dysfunction, the monstrous, the disaster ('Piave', p.43), acts that I fear: "the bridge of your nose will break' ('Next Door Moon', p.14), 'he shoots off   both his hands' ('Her Boyfriend', p.23). My voices, the ones that speak the poems in this section, include dragons ('Wyvern', p.17), people in hell ('Persephone's Refusal', p.19), martyrs on their way to execution ('Investigating the Easter Issue', p.21), an addict ('Bookshelves', p.22), and neckless or serpentine-necked people ('Neck Phase', p.24). All of these problematic individuals and happenings suit, I hope, the variety of form and line that I constructed for them.

CE: You spoke of it taking a whole book to move you out of the primigravida-poet stage. What was your experience of the first book in the world, with your first reviews, shortlisting, launch?

CC: How can you describe that feeling of your progeny being well received? You are delighted but not (I'm being scrupulously honest here) truly surprised. You love your offspring, of course. You want readers to see how marvellous it is! The shortlisting was a particular pleasure because I rate the poets who judged it so highly. Judge Gillian Allnutt had been another inspiration to me. The most important thing to me during the first year of *Stretch of Closures*' life was the friendship it brought with poets whose work I read, but I hadn't known personally before. Roddy Lumsden was one. He was always generous and helped me with my second manuscript. Linda Black was another, still one of the most interesting poets I know, a sophisticated talent.

Also, I could see reviewers were interested in my work. My reviews have been something I've learned from, the good and the not so good. Some writers won't read reviews. I am always interested in feedback. It doesn't change my mind usually, but it expands it. The launch was a joy. I shared it with Jenny Lewis, a brilliant and farsighted poet, who published her first book at the same time. We took over a room at Foyles in Charing Cross Road, a bookshop and a road I love. I was living in London at the time; I felt it was my village and that the villagers had turned out to hear my work.

CE: How do you see the book now, so many years later, in relation to the trajectory your work has taken? What continues, and what has changed?

CC: The major change is that my subsequent books have far tighter overall themes than *Stretch of Closures*. They are also shorter! I don't see that I have changed my style too much, or maybe it's my early voice that is still recognisable. Some poets find their voice after the first one or two collections. Selima Hill is a great example of this, in my view. I think that starting later as a poet meant that my voice was well-established in all parts of my life and my poetry has accommodated it from the start.

REFERENCES

Crowther, C. (2007) *Stretch of Closures*. Exeter: Shearsman Books.
Niedecker, L. (1970) *My Life By Water: Collected Poems 1936–1968*. London, Fulcrum Press.

The Clockwork Gift
(Shearsman, 2009)

CE: The opening poem of your second collection is dedicated to Selima Hill, whom I believe you wrote on as part of your PhD at Kingston University. How would you describe your engagement with Hill's work?

CC: I have been reading Selima Hill's work since her first collection, *Saying Hello at the Station* (Chatto & Windus, 1984). There is something combative about it, a feature that developed more and more through her subsequent collections. I like that and thought of her when I wrote the first line of the opening poem: 'I won't replace lost wedding cutlery' (p.11). I also have a curse poem later in the book ('A Curse on Your Moider', p.78), again influenced by Hill's sure touch with poems that feature an angry or irritable narrator.

I learned from Hill to nurture the surreal. I had surreal leanings from the beginning, but was unsure how to judge the worth of surrealism in a poem. Hill has perfect surreal pitch in my view. Though my poems are not like Hill's, the thike poems in *The Clockwork Gift* are a nod to her surrealism in writing about the problems of an unsociable narrator (pp.27-35). Thikes are invented creatures, not so different to the more familiar dragons and ghosts in other poems in the collection.

Lastly, Hill's work deals with (apparent) autobiography, with poems on the speaker's mother or sister, for example. *The Clockwork Gift* is a collection of poems about grandmothers, a set I had recently joined. I did not want to be particularly autobiographical, but to examine the state of grandmotherhood, and I think that is, to some extent, what Hill is doing in her relationship poems as well.

CE: I'm intrigued by your remarks about Hill's 'combative' quality and use of 'an angry or irritable narrator'. I imagine these qualities manifest tonally and perhaps structurally as well.

CC: One simple example is Hill's method of putting a searing negative inside an everyday image, thus appearing to deflate the negative while amping it up, as here (Hill, p.186):

...suitcases of every description
are leaping up and down in the air
looking like a flock of battered monuments
or bits of bedroom learning how to fly.
And look at yours. It used to be your wife.

If 'your wife' is presented as a suitcase, then the adjective 'battered' is harsh as is the more subtle, but still bruising, description of wives as 'bits of bedroom learning how to fly'; this is a more surreal scene than I would create, but the surprise factor is what I was aiming for in 'Live Grenade in Sack of Potatoes Story': 'Later a police dog bites / his scrotum. I buy chips and biscuits...' (p.12), and in 'Archaeology,' a poem about digging up Grandma's buried body, I wrote: 'We used the big spade or the fork with long tines...' (p.18).

Hill's overall fighting spirit has a different tone to irony, where negatives appear to be positives though the reader knows they are not so positive. In my ten-section poem on St Anne, Jesus's grandmother, there's a battle thread, from Joachim leaving Anne in a threatening environment with dangling wires and blinded windows (p.51), Joachim's teams of Kaons and Pions fighting each other (p.53), through to Jesus's visit to Anne's house imagined on the Somerset Levels: 'The Levels lay exhausted after a licking / from low cloud' (p.60). I wanted to present Anne as a wise older character who would support Joachim and Jesus after their fights and who would offer a nuanced view of battle.

Hill also is a superb deflater; deflation works well within the structure of the very short poem, her signature form. She shrivels the pompous, the overegged, the ambitious. I have a bit of that in this collection, in the four-liner 'St Anne's House' (p.59), or as here, in the eight-line 'Woman, Probably One of the Fates', for example: 'While marble grabs its opportunity / to empty sockets of eyes and teeth – skin is resistance' (p.20). I see the marble statue as presenting a classical, and much vaunted, picture of a personification, whereas skin shows a woman as degradable, temporary and thus a deflation from stone. Yet skin is tough in a very different way to stone.

CE: I love the volta of the last stanza of 'Petra Genetrix', turning from the speaker's relationship to her ancestry to her implied relation to her descendants. What concerns or interests about legacy or inheritance informed your thinking as you worked on this collection?

CC: The grandmother role is one of keeper of the legacy, whether within a family or a larger social group. Grandmothers are the keepers of community wisdom, and they pass on not so much family law and lore as attitudes, defiance or respect depending on the circumstances. It is easy for her to be a teacher because grandmotherhood is a caring role, and children will often mimic their carers; grandmothers play an essential childcare role in contemporary economies, as they have always done. So the legacy is also emotional, or to put it simply, love rather than money. This is what I wanted to express in the second poem in the book, 'Live Grenade in Sack of Potatoes Story'. Children who struggle socially, who are perhaps transgressive and/or outcast, are accepted by the grandmother who does not teach them to tamp down their feelings, but shares their distress: 'They come for my expertise. / It's worth their battering the door / To share my anger. *Nonna, oma, nain.*' (p.12). The three final words are generic names for grandmother, in Italian, German, and Welsh.

Because women have found themselves disinherited, in that women's work, lives and ideas are not canonised in the way that male lives are, the grandmother is hugely important to pass down women's ideas to both women and men.

CE: At what point did it become clear that grandmothering would be a central issue in the book? Once it was, did you actively pursue the issue in your poems?

CC: Very early on. I had written some poems about an older woman ('Ubi Sunt', 'Backpacker') and started to think through the role of grandmother as a special category to which I belonged. I was amazed that a role one has not asked for and has no say in could be so important to one's life and to one's emotions. I adore my grandchildren, but they don't belong to me – the role is humbling and fascinating and made me quite cross to begin with. It was de-stressing to research and write about it.

CE: I know Hobs Moat is a special place for you. Tell me about Hobs Moat and 'The Thike', the creation of this community around a fictional animal.

CC: I was born in a tiny hamlet that had newly grown into a suburb of Solihull/Birmingham, called Hobs Moat. Hob, meaning elf or goblin or mischievous household creature, was first used in the fifteenth century. I also came across a local (Warwickshire) meaning of hob as a small furry animal. I amalgamated the two meanings in my first poem about a thike ('Thike', p.27).

Centuries ago, the moat in the name had surrounded a lost manor house. Now it was empty and dry and the centre of our life as children; we played outdoors, often inside the boundaries of the moat where we were invisible to houses. I felt there was other life there; I couldn't say what, though our parents warned us against strangers who, for reasons I couldn't fathom, might be found in the moat. The thike is a vehicle for social distress in my poems, and I found a freedom in the fact that my readers could not know anything about thikes, so they would have no prejudices about them. Poems are always having to consider streams of reader knowledge, depths of meanings and connotations that words carry. It is extraordinary to use a nonce word in a poem, and you feel you have to earn the right to discountenance a reader like that. After all, a reader will look up the word and not find it; they could feel their time had been wasted.

CE: You mention readers' knowledge and prejudices, and I wonder at what stage in your writing you consider or think about your readers, and how that influences your work. Admittedly, perhaps you can only answer this in regard to yourself now rather than the poet you were when you wrote *The Clockwork Gift*....

CC: This is an essential question, one that I'm asked repeatedly, and I sense that there are poems I've written that appear not to consider the reader very much in that they seem inaccessible. When I'm asked, I say either 'Never' or 'All the time'. 'Never' because from the first to last in writing a poem I'm listening – I'm not sure to what or to who but listening is the only way I can describe how I write. So, to think of a reader would stop me listening, it would be a different mental activity, and I'd lose focus and then not know how to complete the poem. This listening, which is so reader-indifferent, may relate to the experience North American poet Jack Spicer described in his mid-twentieth-century lectures; he said poets are like radio receivers. I don't want to use the word inspired, but there has been a tradition of picturing a poet as led by a muse. A muse is not a reader. When I say 'All the time', I mean I'm conscious at every step of the writing process that I'm using a language, words, grammatical constructions, and those things are a group consensus, tools to communicate, so I'm completely aware that I'm communicating and half the fun is to wield language in subtle and unexpected ways.

My problem with readers is assuming that what is fun for me is fun for them. Maybe it is, maybe not. But I have to share the joke. My poems always play. I've changed in my attitude to readers since the beginning of my poetry journey by accepting that readers differ and change their perceptions at various stages of reading. So, even more than formerly, I don't try to adjust for the 'ideal' reader. I don't think my style has changed at all, but there are aspects of it which are more widely liked now or more fashionable: wordplay, for example. That's lucky for me.

CE: 'The Herebefore' (p.40) feels like the book's pivot, a consideration of the legacy of the past and how we bring it into the present. Would you speak a little of the poem's development?

CC: I wrote that poem in bits and pieces, over two years, while reading about and considering grandmotherhood. I felt it come to life when I was standing on a bridge above a little weir in a field near Glastonbury where I was living at the time. I felt the grandmother persona was speaking to me (p.41):

> *In no-man's land meet me, set me a time:*
> *the lattermath of war.* There I rock on the steel,
> slit to ribbons above powered pleats of water
> falling weeded from the mirage of still pool
>
> to its spun slip of lace torn off by black ground.

That's an accurate description of the weir; I can see it now. I was scribbling in my notebook and had no idea how I would use this description. Back at home, it was obvious. It would be in such a rural setting that I would meet my grandmother, my 'herebefore', because one of my grandmothers lived in such a setting all her life and the other was born in one.

After writing those central stanzas, I felt I understood that the poem was a celebration of the meeting we make with our antecedents somewhere in our psyche. Then I could piece it all together and depict a seemingly fabled unreal character more fully. One of my grandmothers did write poetry, informally and unpublished, and the sole memento I have is a copy of Robert Browning's poem 'My Last Duchess' bound by her in leather.

CE: I can see a similarity in your and Browning's work in the use of a slowly developing argument, aided by a subtle rhetoric. Of the canonical poets, whom do you feel has most inspired or influenced your work, and how has this manifested in your poems?

CC: I read Browning extensively many years ago and loved his abrupt rhythms; I loved it specifically because it was anything but mellifluous whereas his Victorian contemporaries had a near-universal sweetness of rhythm. For the same reason I loved Donne whose work strays into metrical nonsense (mere syllabicism!) where he judges it necessary.

Both of them build an argument as the *raison d'être* of each poem, implying that there has to be thought for a poem to exist. I agree with that and with Don Paterson who said, I'm not sure where, quoting I.A. Richards (Richards, 1930, p.1), that a poem (Richards says a book) is a machine for thinking with. Perhaps fleshing out a thought or a thought process in words is as much what poetry does as realising emotion and sensation in words. Terrance Hayes uses the machine image for the craft of a poem and compares that with the life of the poem: 'if a poem is a machine, it's an animal too ... I think the poem is mostly an animal' (2023, p.42). The canonical poets who have influenced me clearly show the 'animal heart of the machine shell' (p.42). Gerard Manley Hopkins is another such. I learned from his poetry how to fuse wild rhythm, extravagant line and extraordinary content and how to do that with as much intellectual rigour as I could. I still strive for that effect. Not that I use Hopkins's sprung rhythm, it's more the mad metaphor and tsunamic roar of lines coming at the meaning that I'm after. Of course, you might not recognise Hopkins in my work because I don't end up where I set off to go, if that makes sense. But I keep a talismanic Hopkins poem, 'Spring and Fall', in my head most of the time I write. I learned this poem when I was eleven. In my latest collection, *Solar Cruise*, the poem 'Worlds of Wanwood' is a homage to it (p.56).

A poet whose work has had an influence on my poetic attitude – how I talk to the reader – is Stevie Smith. Her poems and novels are playful but make serious points. For example her legendary line 'not waving but drowning', is devastating because the subject of the poem is dying but also comic: 'poor chap he always loved larking / and now he's dead.' (Smith, 2015, p.347). I felt encouraged by her bravery in making much of her poetry insouciant as opposed to solemn and, while I'm not a comic poet or even a satirical poet, if I want to laugh at something, including myself, I will. I'd say 'A Curse on Your Moider' and 'Backpacker', among others in *The Clockwork Gift*, owe a debt of tone to Stevie Smith. Here's a hint of Smith's wryness in 'Backpacker': 'rare as an egg / laid by a leatherback turtle, she smiles / through the bars of a waterfront jail in Bocas' (p.64).

CE: In the second half of *The Clockwork Gift*, where the speaker more consistently appears in the same character, the character appears both as a grandmother and a witty, intelligent person independent of that role. What would you say of your portrayal of grandmothers both across the collection and in the second section? How is that portrayal informed by your use of diction, syntax, cultural references, etc.?

CC: The first half is more fable and wisdom than depictions of specific grannies. In the second half, though I do have a Baba Yaga poem (granny as a powerful threat), I wanted to show some recognisable everyday negatives (or what is seen as negative in a society that idealises women and particularly caring women), even in the streetwise and highly active women I was meeting, in person and in people's memories. 'Postwar' describes a young woman dressing to kill in the 'forties, while 'Backpacker' depicts a newly freed older woman travelling abroad. I picture one grandmother as an old battery (a place where weaponry was stored), another as a decaying car, another as a funfair closed for winter. But there is a central fable in the second half, the story of St Anne, Jesus's grandmother. These poems vary, in cultural reference and therefore in diction, and that leads me to vary the syntax. 'Fatality' uses the terminology of cars and the working garage: '*chatterhop,* what damaged wipers do' (p.71). Grandmother, a woman seen as damaged beyond repair to young people, is seen as a broken windscreen through the eyes of a car mechanic. I imagine a Victorian grandmother joining in a game of street football and making the winning catch, despite her mockery by a neighbour. The period names of local people and street machinery are fascinating: 'Dust Destructor', 'Master Woodger' (p.49). Syntactically, I use various tactics to support the approach to age in each poem. There are long streams of clauses, which is one way to depict the length of age. 'Thirteen' is a short poem with two-line stanzas of one short line followed by a one-word line, almost always a verb. This depicts the life of a grandson and the poem ends on an adjective 'open': a grandson is open-ended, a granny is not.

CE: How did it feel to move from your first to your second collection of poems?

CC: There is a feeling with a first collection that you are climbing a mountain, and you just have to get to the peak. But when you do, the view is of more mountain peaks. And that is a strange place to stand. You have to make a decision: do I carry on climbing or go back down? After all, you have done what you set out to do. When *Stretch of Closures* had been published and the excitement of the launch and readings was over, I remember, after a lot of thought, making a conscious choice to carry on writing poetry. Writing poetry takes huge commitment in my case because my process is lengthy, not to say unwieldy and antisocial (if I have to get down a version at 3 a.m., so be it). Writing the first draft of a new poem is compulsive though, while making a poem come good is not compulsive, more a matter of steely will. Collections (I have now written six) typically take me about four years to complete.

The Clockwork Gift was the result of making a career choice. From now on, poetry was going to be the lead job in my life. In fact, I stepped away from a good job and signed on for an MPhil followed by a PhD, to ensure I had the skills to write critical work and also so that somebody somewhere was expecting me to show them a poem on a regular basis.

CE: You wrote *The Clockwork Gift* as part of your PhD in Creative Writing. How did composing a manuscript as part of an academic programme affect the creative process?

CC: I did approach the book differently from my first collection in that I was determined to foreground research in my process: I read about grandmotherhood historically and sociopolitically as well as making my own observations of a wider set of contemporary grandmothers.

Had I been writing as I did for *Stretch of Closures,* I would have worked mainly from my personal experience (though the resulting poems are not autobiographical). Through the PhD, I learned how to write poetry as a well-informed witness rather than (or as well as) from within my own life. There's a play between academic research and creative energy. Perhaps because of that training, I would not revise a poem without reading as far as possible around the subjects that emerged in the poem.

Undercutting the academic approach while still using it, I enjoyed writing 'Sleeping on a Trampoline', which creates apparent and imaginary academic references (p.32):

> It was a common word once. Pepys' diary,
> earliest known mention, bar mummers' plays:
> *Home where the thike is come out of the country.*
>
> Keats' letter: *I think upon crutches like the thikes*
> *in your Pump Room.* Matthew Arnold, a rare
> attempt at definition: *Thikes were boys*
>
> *whose good character was easily regressed.*
> Monk Lewis: *She wasn't conversational. Whether shy*
> *or as a result of her theikism, no one could tell.*

That is a poem that I possibly wouldn't have written without some academic experience. It gave me permission, having done a slew of reading about historical and contemporary social judgments, to offer a satirical example of the poor academic practice of selecting statements to fit a theory. Some readers have read this poem and assumed, given my evidence, that thikes exist. As they do, I would say.

CE: *The Clockwork Gift* is as much about age as about grandmothers, about the loss of youth. How did this elegiac element emerge as you worked on the book?

CC: Yes, it's fair to say the book is an apprehension of the horror story that ageing presents. Check the recurring words: ruin, decay, haunt, ghost, skull, dead/death/dying. There is a wide exploration of ageing by other poets, but I sympathise with Ruth Fainlight who says, in her poem 'Ageing', that she started exploring age in her forties and, at a more advanced age, ran out of things to say (2010, p.30). It seemed to me while I wrote *The Clockwork Gift* that I could dispose of the burden of age and from then on write with less of a feeling that I have half left the world.

This is why I wrote the final poem, 'A Seafront Wake for the Postwar', as my final statement on the ageing of my own generation (p.79):

My time was blonde scraped up in a froth. Now our white hair
is arranged against purple. From birth, the agenda of regeneration
confuses us. 'Skip it.'

I read future time by Attlee as surely as if those clock hands, beamed
on the wake wall from a light disguised as a camera, are snapping
facts. All of it is skin

though now it shakes loose of flesh, once stock still like rock inside.

Of course, it hasn't been my final statement. I hear ageing in every moment that I 'listen' while I write, and I see it in every image that gives itself to the poem I'm writing. It's fearful but the increased awareness of psychic depth is worth the fear of standing on a cliff edge, knowing I must jump, and soon.

References

Crowther, C. (2009) *The Clockwork Gift*. Exeter: Shearsman Books.
Crowther, C. (2020) *Solar Cruise*. Bristol: Shearsman Books.
Fainlight, R. (2010) *New and Collected Poems*. Tarset: Bloodaxe Books.
Hayes, T. (2023) *Watch Your Language*. New York: Penguin Books.
Hill, S. (1984) *Saying Hello at the Station*. London: Chatto & Windus.
Hill, S. (2008) *Gloria*. Tarset: Bloodaxe Books.
Richards, I. A. (1930) *Principles of Literary Criticism*. London: Kegan Paul.
Smith, S. (2015) *The Collected Poems & Drawings of Stevie Smith*. London: Faber & Faber.

On Narrowness
(Shearsman, 2015)

CE: *On Narrowness* opens with brio with your Jabberwocky-inspired 'The Alices', and later the abecedarian 'UFood' delights in the sonic play of nonsense words. I'd be interested to hear more about these poems as well as your interest in Nonsense poems more broadly.

CC: For a long while I've been interested in the way nonsense works for poetry. Firstly, poems can be very powerful on a sound level, with specific meanings taking second place. Part of my process with a poem is to learn the poem at some point in its development, recite it aloud, and then it needs to impress me with its rhythms. Choruses often take off and out of meaning and into an incantation that can seem surreal.

Secondly, a poet can take meaning and subvert it without losing it, to be funny or to be challenging. I think Wallace Stevens does that. His poems may sound like nonsense but aren't usually. Thirdly, a poet can simply deny meaning as much as possible to liberate the reader from having to think analytically. All these things are done with words, and the nonsense words may stay with a reader longer than sensible ones. That's because an effective poem wakes a reader up with words that seem not to be what the reader has heard before: not nonsense necessarily or even usually, but not the sense you're used to. I love playing with these boundaries, moving towards the unexpected or skirting round the obvious or pushing the reader right through into the dark wood of nonsense.

'The Alices' suggests a cover up and also a need to speak of what is socially unsayable: for example, we are manipulative as a species, and we are also enablers (p.11). I wanted to write in a tired-of-it-all tone and didn't want that to sound simply patronising or detached. I opted for a tone of personal confusion and minor irritation. Borrowing nonce words from Lewis Carroll lent me that tone. 'Mome', for example, according to Humpty Dumpty in *Through the Looking-Glass*, means the characters 'had lost their way' (Dean, 1997, no pagination). So there are meanings in the poem but a reader should feel a bit freer to bring their own meaning to it.

I wrote 'UFood' as an effusion of words, because I like the way nonsense can be pure play while delivering its meaning. I had done a reading at Lancaster Festival with Geraldine Monk. I had read Geraldine's work previously, but never met her; she is delightful, witty and terrific company. We had dinner afterwards, and next day on the train, thinking back over the meal and the conversation, I wrote the poem and used the abecedarian, each line starting with the next letter of the alphabet, to tie its effusion down. Geraldine is a poet who is not easily boundaried by poetic convention, so you could say I was inspired by her. Being inspired is an historic way to speak apparent nonsense while speaking a deeper truth than normal. I can't claim that for my nonsense work, but I do have an idea that it sometimes helps me get at the experience of reality a bit more closely than conventional words can.

CE: You say you used the abecedarian to 'tie [the poem's] effusion down'. Does form provides a channel for or shape an 'effusion' or idea?

CC: I prefer to think of form as part of the shaping process. I don't think of meaning as the liquor in the bottle; I think of a poem as a piece of sculpture, indivisible, meaning, form, content, words. 'Effusion' means, to me, the process of writing the piece into being. As I write I am creating a firework display in my mind, and on the page, and I need to freeze that, mid-air if possible.

CE: The opening three poems all touch on female characters speaking against constraint. Is this a way of presenting one aspect of the relevance of the collection's title, *On Narrowness*?

CC: Yes, the title indicates constraint, and the poems (the whole collection, I hope) interpret constraint as both problematic and enabling. A conundrum, actually. I think the Oulipians, who believe imposing a constraint on a piece of writing improves it, have a point. Anyway, all poems are constrained, of course: lines, metres, syllables, the page, the breath, the life experience of the poet. But I enjoyed writing about that sense of being cuffed, of being slowed, of being framed, etc. Women have particular and overheavy experience of constraint. 'Captured Women' describes women who are not only socially delineated but also physically framed, since they are pictures. In 'Coincidence of Bodies', the speaker (a female astronomer) addresses the way women's constrained space can express individuality (p.14):

> The heavier I was, the more I shaped space
> round me. Mass curves space. Come on eclipses, you never
> could have blocked me. I curved new space.

Later in the collection, 'Jehanne d'Arc and the Angels of Battle' makes the same point, as do 'Legend of Grey' and 'A Wanderer in End Erring Wood'. The protagonists of those poems are struggling to free themselves in some way.

CE: I found interesting the rhythms created by 'Ad Astra', with its short lines to the right of the longer, flush-left lines, and 'Snow at Christmas', which similarly alternates very short with longer lines, but all flush left. What led you to these shapings and rhythms for these poems?

CC: Two things push me to play with the very short/much longer line pattern: sound/rhythm as you suggest and also position on the page. The mind, which I hope is singing along with the words on the page, encounters a space, a stop, and halts the song being sung. I always try to make the last word or words of a line particularly important – unless they are unimportant connecting words such as 'has', 'to', used for an important reason (as in 'The Candidate Goes Home'). Endings are usually a subtle blow to the reading brain! But if I want to increase the impact, I pull out the last words so that they hang in space.

'Ad Astra' ends with a 'startling' effect that I saw in the Italian bay where Shelley drowned. It was early afternoon, and the glitter from the sea was almost violent. I made pages of notes describing it, and when I wrote the poem, I began with the ending, a sense of light striking the sea, and worked back to the beginning of the poem. Thus, the strike effect, which I hoped to get from each stanza having a pulled-out first and last line-ending, appeared from the first stanza, as here (p.20):

> So strongwilled, the thumb of the sun
>   On sea,
> [...]
> Sea waves to swink blank swink blank
>   Swink blank.

I wanted the stanzas to flick on and off, but not to be simply visually appealing (I like the look of hanging words that rhyme and chime with each other): I wanted them to poke the reader in the eye just as it's almost painful to look at an intense sun-on-wave glitter. So the last two outlying line endings are 'I think' and 'swink-blank', hard single-syllable words. The last word of the poem is 'blank' (p.20). It leaves an empty page below it. The sun has stopped working its display on the waves. The poem is over.

'Snow at Christmas' has a different impact, I hope. It addresses the way Christmas masks real and not always kind human behaviour. I intended the very short lines to suggest falling snow – two syllables fall at the beginning of alternate lines. These are mostly gentle-sounding and gentle-meaning words: 'welcome', 'and shy'. The poem finishes on a short line, 'and love', but it begins with the violence that Christmas rejects: 'snow as a raptor', 'a dog that bites / a child'. Finally the unacceptable sentiments of hate and cultural kitsch resolve by the repudiation of culture and an address to reality (pp.58-59):

> We haven't read a word
> since then
> all Christmas but proper names, prepositions
> and love.

The short ending line flush left in traditional fashion is the word that should mean what Christmas is touted as meaning – if it ever can.

CE: 'The Night of Misrule' and 'The Night Bacchus Let Us Down' seem to take us from a Nonsense poetry of linguistic invention to narrative whimsy. Would you tell me about these poems' inspirations and motives?

CC: I occasionally like to create the voice of the village storyteller. I spent an afternoon in a small community in Italy; perhaps I was told ('The Night of Misrule') or I overheard ('The Night Bacchus Let us Down') a local story. Is it true? Yes and no. There should be inventiveness in a story, but there should also be some truth to the local history that inspires it. 'The Night of Misrule' is set in an Italian village on an Italian plain. This village – I've forgotten its name and wouldn't want to quote it anyway since the poem might be taken for a purely local account when it is my own invention – was having a gourd festival. Pumpkins were displayed in all their splendour on stalls packing the narrow streets. Donkeys wandered round holding adverts for local sellers of mushrooms or huge tomatoes. The variety of colours and species of gourds enthralled me. I spent hours making notes, and the story subsequently wrote itself. That is to say, I didn't extend the narrative particularly when I honed the poem later. If it's whimsical, the place is not. The growers and sellers were highly professional. However, I do believe in 'nonsense' narration, storytelling without needing narrative to be realistic.

'The Night Bacchus Let us Down' is set in a gated community that I lived in a long while ago. I had a sort of shock on the day I moved in: I couldn't find the code to unlock the large entry gates. When I was rescued by the gardener and the gates swung shut behind me, I felt that being locked in was worse than being locked out. The response you might make to that experience, of being in a gated community, is to cast it as nonsense: how can it be rational to lock ourselves up? It feels like fear. It does not feel peaceful. Nonsense keeps a humorous head above its anxiety: the paper-woman who leaves freesheets outside the gate is a god, compared to us within (p.32):

> ...as surely
> as she is nameless and her russet dust
> hanging in our mouths isn't drinkable
> so all our imperfections are invisible
> to her.

I thought I would celebrate the community by inventing a nonsense night that even Bacchus, god of conviviality, doesn't want to attend. In the end, at the end of the poem, the place is upside down, as are its inhabitants: 'Watch our wings fin through this airy salt' (p.32).

CE: This book feels like an investigation of interwoven threads, such as the issues of what constitutes nonsense, the extent to which women can speak, etc. Would you tell me about the investigations, explorations, considerations you were engaged with in the course of *On Narrowness*?

CC: During the years that it took to complete this collection, I thought deeply about the functions of poetry and the tasks of a poet: for example, witnessing (see my answer below), resurrecting the lost or the dead, giving voice to the voiceless including objects and the natural world, showing emotion as a political force. It was as though my third collection had to be justified. Previously I had not questioned the value of spending huge amounts of time writing, rewriting, etc. I didn't think I needed a reason to write; indeed, I usually decided to write when I had moved past thinking I could help anyone or save anything by writing. I needed to feel there was no point in my writing the next few lines for me to be able to write them. Pointlessness suited me. Yet for this collection, while I still needed nonsense to free me to write, I and my subject matter became more self-consciously sociopolitical. This is partly to do with ageing as such and ageing as a poet. (Sometimes in denial of ageing – as in 'Young winds I think like you.' (p.24). No, really, I don't.) As well as trying to serve those purposes I listed, the poems concern self-assessment: from 'The Alices' to 'Emotion at Work' to 'Who Was I?' I don't come up with any answers, of course; that isn't the role of poetry. It's all still a blur: 'I try to think a poem through glaze. It fails' ('Gold Moment', p.63), or, in 'Self-Portrait as Windscreen' (p.42):

> Do you think I'm clear on every issue
> just because I'm glass?
> Have you heard yourself calling 'Claire,
>
> Claire, Claire, Claire,' when you're confused?

CE: I read 'The Witness' again a few months after George Floyd's killing, where he protested to police he couldn't breathe, exactly like your suspect in the poem. Can you tell me about the work of witnessing in this poem and the significance of the fossils the speaker sees on later revisiting the scene?

CC: Witnessing is an important job that many poets do well, and it is a civic duty for all of us. 'The Witness' relates, and resituates, an incident that happened to someone close to me (the witness is not the subject of police harassment). The subject of harassment was allowed to leave the scene when the witness announced to the police that she would stand and be a witness. It was the declaration of the act of witnessing that determined the outcome. It seemed to me that, if I witnessed in a poem her witnessing in a street situation, I could draw attention to the act of witnessing itself.

CE: Does 'Infatible' mark the beginning of your interest in the *fatras*? How did you first encounter the form?

CC: I can't remember how I came across the fatras; I think I was researching something to do with Nonsense poetry and came across this mediaeval form. A fatras is a French thirteenth- and fourteenth-century Nonsense poem, much loved by the aristocracy. It began as the fatrasie, a short Nonsense poem with a very precise form: a strict rhyme scheme, a strict syllabic and line count. There should be eleven lines preceded by a couplet formed of the first and last lines of the main strophe. During the thirteenth century the fatrasie extended its range to include pious and rational subject matter as well as nonsense. It's this later phase that I pay homage to in my versions. I ignore the syllable and line count, but stick to eleven lines preceded by the first line/last line couplet. There is something magical about the first and last lines encapsulating a whole poem. I also found something magical about the word 'fatras' when I used the form for a set of poems about body fat – a wordplay not appreciated by some reviewers. But I used it in the spirit of the Nonsense history of the form. I make my own pun in the invented word 'infatible' and draw attention to it with the lines 'I've always thought / over is almost all of lover.' (p.66). Since then I use the fatras regularly because sometimes I need to make a set of repeating words that become more complex by the end of the poem. This is not the same as an epiphany; it's closer to the nature of reflection. Words and phrases you think you understand become amplified if you listen. A fatras helps you to listen to words more closely.

CE: You mention that your wordplay was 'not appreciated by some reviewers', and I wonder how you regard reviews, what their relevance is to your process, perhaps.

CC: I do read reviews when I come across them. I always find them encouraging and, where the reviewer goes into depth, useful as a way of knowing whether my meanings are being picked up or perhaps other meanings I hadn't thought of are coming across. I don't think any review has altered my practice, but some have been illuminating about my formal approaches. I hadn't thought of myself as an elliptical poet until a reviewer used the phrase.

Occasionally, reviews give me other ideas. I was once reviewed twice for the same book because the reviewer thought about the book after completing the first review and wanted to say more about it. That taught me to read other poets' work more than once and with a gap between readings. Apart from when I'm studying a text or reviewing it myself, I was surprised to realise how often I simply read a collection once. The result is that I have a roomful of poetry books because, to read in depth and over time, you have to own the book.

References

Crowther, C. (2015) *On Narrowness*. Bristol: Shearsman Books.
Dean, C. (1997) *The Jabberwocky*. Available at: https://www.alice-in-wonderland.net/resources/analysis/interpretive-essays/the-jabberwocky/ (accessed: 9 February 2024).

Solar Cruise
(Shearsman, 2020)

CE: Let's begin with the title page: the book is called *Solar Cruise* with the subtitle *A Memoir*. Can you tell me about the decision to include that subtitle, to call a collection of poetry a memoir?

CC: That decision came late in the development of *Solar Cruise*. I had been sketching out the history of a physicist who becomes aware of the power of physics to affect the future of a climate-challenged world, and I was also describing the new physics relevant to provision of future-conscious fuel. As the poems grew towards each other – this being an inevitable process when you write a set of poems around themed subject matter – they increasingly reflected the conversations from which they were derived. For almost every poem, I had to talk to my partner, physicist Keith Barnham, about his work, his discovery and development of the quantum solar cell, his history as a particle physicist. Getting him to sit down and give me the large quantities of question time that I needed was fraught.

I was perhaps halfway through this MS when we needed to go to the USA. We decided to do the trip without flying – so we went by boat and train. During the voyage, my partner agreed to devote three hours a day to growing the poems with me. By this stage he was anxious to make sure the physics was correct, of course. The eight-day voyage became a retreat for us, and it gave us time to reflect on our own relationship, our callings as scientist and writer, our history as a partnership as well as his history. I began to foreground our relationship, as well as my own growing understanding of solar physics, in the poems.

At last the work became a long poem about the voyage we had taken. The cabin became the heart of our work, a sort of Vulcan's cave – the deck, surrounded by unfathomable ocean, became an invite into an imaginary world. At the end of the voyage, I felt my MS was also finished even if it needed polishing. So I called it a memoir.

CE: With the use of narrative through the collection, the approach to titling palpably changes, becoming more decidedly contextualising and, interestingly, more playful – I'm thinking of such splendid titles as

'Harvest in the Quantum Well Solar Cell Reminds Me of Lipstick', 'The Ghost of Marie Curie Works Up a Chorus while Chatting to Enthusiasts at a Model Engine Rally in 2015', and 'The First Criticisms Every Solar Sceptic Makes Drive a Physicist-Loving Poet to Doggerel'. Did you compose the titles at the same time as the poems, or did they come later, as you brought the manuscript together? How were you thinking of the titles' role in the manuscript, particularly given its operating as a larger narrative or memoir?

CC: The process was a mixture of serious needs: to help the reader understand what the poem would be about and to reflect the fun I was having with the process of uncovering these lines. I did have tremendous fun with this book. This might have been a hysterical reaction to the horror of a world where climate change is allowed to carry on unchecked. There is a huge amount of frustration in trying to push the world in a certain direction. Often, the cabin would steam with hot profanities. Letting off steam was essential. That's partly the source of 'Cabin Coffin'. For me as a poet, the titles were a way to warn a reader, a preliminary cool-off, before the poem launches its diatribe. But also I am a mature observer. It's an age thing – I have seen intentions go cold, disintegrate, reassemble, disintegrate again. I've been tormented by beliefs – like the goodness of human beings. Humour has become a way to, inside myself, deal with the world and survive taking humanity seriously.

Some titles, though, introduce a poem in which I take the torment on its own tough terms: 'Heart Cut Out of the Sun' uses an early twentieth-century murder story to image the wrench of my partner's heart on those occasions when his work and ideas are rejected. I illustrate that poem with a photo of the solar cell he invented on his palm. Titles do set a tone. This is all serious material – and there are other serious titles – 'Genia in Memoriam', for example, or 'Think Workers'.

CE: You make a pointed reference to the use of syllabics in 'She Counts, He Counts'; here it appears a way to compare the work of the poet and the physicist. Could you say more about that relationship between science and poetry, so central to *Solar Cruise*, and, if relevant, how syllabics figures in that relationship?

CC: Both roles, poet and physicist, are important to society. Both physicists and poets use maths, or ordered ways to interpret the world if you like. I wanted to make this point. I chose syllabics in many of the poems for another, tangential reason: syllabics has not been a popular formal way to construct a poem. Nor, usually, is ground-breaking physics that doesn't contribute to political imperatives. I myself love syllabics and admire several contemporary syllabic poets' work.

To call oneself a syllabicist is a bit like calling oneself a physicist. Who assumes a physicist is only a physicist? Clearly my partner is a former of futures, a philosopher, a prophet, a creator of new physical forms, etc., etc. So also poets who count do more than count. And both of us count for more because we relate to each other and support each other, formally speaking.

CE: Continuing on the relationship between the role of the poet and the role of the physicist, I wonder if your long interest in nonsense poetry has a role here, too.

CC: Some of the poems veer towards nonsense tropes ('Debate on a Private Deck' or 'After Dinner Speaker') or forms ('Wingding'). To a non-physicist, the material discoveries of particle science or solar science, the two areas my partner has worked in, sound like nonsense: the Higgs boson is a particle that has always died before you reach it, before you even glimpse it. The inventions experimental physicists make are equally odd: fields in solar farms grow rows of panels in huge shiny leaves. The physicist might not notice the oddity of these creations and inventions, but a poet might. Similarly a scientist might think lineating a description of the basic norms of solar energy ('OK Professor') is odd. Either way, poetry can draw attention to the strange new world we have to inhabit if we are to create a less destructive physics. Physics has been tolerant of environmental danger, nuclear physics for example. It has not been committed to usefulness, and it has been, perhaps unintentionally, esoteric.

The process of intuition and drive that creates new physics and new poems can be narrated as near-nonsense ('The Crystallier') because it is beyond reason, having to bring to light what has never been thought. The politics of climate change is often as nonsensical as it is horrifying. So I refer to a nonsense character: Sir Dogrel Olkincole satirises those funders of energy development who prefer fossil fuel to cleaner solar energy. I have invented a prophetic epigraph to the book written by a nonsense character Hurtle B. Hurtle on his website www.blogspew.com: 'Physics is S.S. Eschatology'.

CE: Toward the end, *Solar Cruise* feels increasingly elegiac, contemplating the potential for the speaker's loss and the meaning of that loss. 'Salt' is a particularly powerful celebration of marriage, following on the heels of the speaker's plan at the end of 'Becalmed' with its epigraph '*a prehumous song*', 'But if your love/ take him, take me' (2020, p.66).

CC: Inevitably, voyages end. Even if only one of us should get off the boat, the relationship would be over. 'Becalmed' is an attempt to infuse an ending with the power of relationship, the discoveries made in a relationship. 'Darklight' is a term I use for solar power, as used by my partner; it's a term that could suggest an ending. The speaker of that poem is asking for more knowledge; it's not all over yet (p.66):

> Darklight, darklight,
> our light, our dark,
> if there is more
> for us to sense
>
> shake out your grains
> of star and park
> the continents.
> So let us stare
>
> becalmed offshore.

So the 'love' of the last line is not simply death but also commitment to more research, more work for the good of the future world.

'Salt' is celebratory of marriage, but I hope the term 'marriage' can be thought of as wider than usual; 'a marriage of true minds' takes place wherever thinkers/creative workers join in a shared vision and elaborate that vision together. After 'Salt', there is 'Transtraditional Atlantic', a poem of reckoning, a look to what we have achieved or failed to achieve (2020, p.69):

Physicist, is it over?

Poet, how strong
a voyage have you sung

to powerfill an ocean?

The problem in writing about a relationship based on striving toward a massive and complex goal is how to be truthful about limits; my partner is very good at this. Failure is built into any endeavour just as death is into life. I wanted *Solar Cruise* to be upbeat; to me, this way of life is the best way. But it's hard to celebrate being cut off before you complete a task, which you must be, as a scientist, and I think, as a poet also. So some of the humour in the book is ironic.

CE: Thinking about the project of *Solar Cruise*, do you consider yourself an ecopoet? Do you anticipate returning to this material in some way again in the future?

CC: It's hard to avoid eco dimensions to a poem now. In my time as a poet, I think ecological consciousness has developed and strengthened in poetry. I've always thought of myself as an edgelands poet or, since this is where I've always lived, a less cool sub-urban poet. I'm not sure there's a real division between town and country anyway. In the inner and outer parts of towns and cities, there are numerous beasts and plants, only a fraction of which are human. They coexist and affect each other. They must use each other carefully or face mixed consequences. Even inside the body, any sort of living body, the microbiota is managing its territory. I'm aware humans have been managing their territory poorly and that knowledge affects my poetry. From time to time, my poems have been overt about this.

As far as the eco-problems my partner works with, I might well find they impact on poems of mine that are not directly addressing them. Or I might find the courage to set off toward a different focus on solar energy. Light drives life, grows plants, evolves plants to animals: electromagnetic light stimulates that process. One of the great coincidences of life is that the most intense light beams are the golden ones, from the sun. These are the beams that stimulated evolution. But the eco-solar poetry I would write would focus on human life, as *Solar Cruise* does. I'd like to write about the physicality of ageing. I'm interested in how light interacts with physical change. Light is an electromagnetic wave, not always a gentle one, but a positive force in us until our death, the absence of light. While we are living, we radiate electromagnetism. The sun and other stars are integral to every day of our life.

I have written some poems about this, in collections before *Solar Cruise*. 'Coincidence of Bodies' from *On Narrowness* is one, a poem in the post-death voice of Beatrice Tinsley, an astronomer who died young (2015, p.14):

> And if I'd survived till fallen flesh
> changed my shape so it wasn't hunted or held up, would I
> have resolved the paradox of flesh –
>
> that I was made of more than I am?
> Mars, you wore only a helmet half off to show us flesh
> is too frail for battle. My fabric now
>
> is lighter than flesh, the blue of galaxies.
> I am what has been proved of the coincidence of bodies,
> given I'm not shortlived and can eclipse.

I'd like to write more about mortal change in our new, possibly apocalyptic, organic world. To do that, I've used physics in my current collection *A Pair of Three*. Here are lines from two poems that depict a human relationship, 'The Physics of Coincidence' (2022, p.24):

> If two atoms
>
> share an electron and bond in one body
> in one compass-
> ion of matter swaying with so much co-
> incidence direct-
>
> ionless as the atoms that long for time
> to herd its lengths
> into shocks that rope and weave each to each…
> then there's no which.

and 'Mussels at Fisherman's Wharf' (2022, p.25): 'While Keith dreams of sun and her, I dream / dark matter can stream memories from tachyons / that glow and flow to and fro in soul physics.'

I view my poetics of ecology in general and physics in particular as what you might call *transwriting*. The word *transreading* means reading a poem slowly to make a cultural and literal language translation. Transwriting I use to mean the creation of a complex of literal scientific references and cultural applications of science written in a poet's personal language with its emotional arteries. Perhaps that makes me a biopoet.

REFERENCES

Crowther, C. (2015) *On Narrowness*. Bristol: Shearsman Books.
Crowther, C. (2020) *Solar Cruise*. Bristol: Shearsman Books.
Crowther, C. (2022) *A Pair of Three*. Bristol: Shearsman Books.

A Pair of Three
(Shearsman, 2022)

CE: There's an elegance in the movement at the beginning of *A Pair of Three* from the dedication, to your husband's first wife (though another reader would be unlikely to know that at that point), to your opening eponymous poem establishing the collection's focus, on what might be thought of as a three-way marriage – your husband's with his previous wife and you. What led you to this focus? Did you feel any unease about tackling such a potentially unwieldy topic?

CC: If I had thought ahead, I might have baulked at the complications I would need to communicate in poetry about a situation such as this. But, over time, poems come as they will, and I don't work out how they are related until I notice a set of poems forming. Then I take months – years in some cases – to understand and clarify exactly what the set is about. It is an exciting moment when I realise. At that point, I go through the set adjusting the poems so that they fit the theme more clearly. That's a good redraft because, by then, I will have become too familiar with the poems to see their flaws. Having a deeper understanding of their connection allows me to draft much more carefully.

For example, 'Mussels at Fisherman's Wharf' is a poem that seemed to me initially to be about an extraordinary scientist, Gerson Goldhaber, and his work. I couldn't understand, at first, why I wanted to set the poem in San Francisco Bay. Though that is where I first met Gerson, that setting seemed at odds with or just distracting from the scientific aura I wanted to dominate the poem. Once I had realised that I was writing a set of poems about my partner's lost love, I grasped straightaway that the science of destiny was of huge importance to the poem, and also that Keith and Jude had lived near San Francisco and had had their first child there. I then cut out some of the explanatory science I had included, replacing it with a description of the bay itself and its living creatures. Writing about a theme is a process of discovery for me, and a theme seems less something decided upon beforehand than something uncovered.

CE: The cover description calls *A Pair of Three* your 'most personal [collection] yet', and by that it clearly means *explicitly* personal, as personal interests and experiences have rivered throughout your work. Did you have a sense of writing more openly or exposedly in this work, and if so, how did that influence your poetics?

CC: For me, personal can mean the acceptable public face of one's own life or the interior vulnerable part of my being that I have always kept very private. You could argue that poetry is better for taking the risk of opening up. Confessional poetry is an example of that. But even such overtly personal poetry as, for example, the early work of Sharon Olds, is structured as a narrative, a story, and I feel that protects the writer. For me, there is always a 'once upon a time' feeling to a poem, even one that describes an actual event. Yet there is widespread interpretation of poems, among non-poet readers, as autobiographical. I have always believed that all poetry is a fiction, and much of my poetry is imaginary from its conception, bearing no relationship to real life events. Even where it uses real-life material, I am perfectly able to change the data in a poem so that, if the person who sparked off my initial draft read it, they would not recognise their agency in it or at least would understand that I am not writing about them as such. Yet in *A Pair of Three*, once I understood what I was writing about, I decided to pull away that defence and make everything in the collection actual and accurate to my experience, even the dreams, even the intimate poems. Nothing is fiction here. I could have worked on such autobiographical poems as I usually do, by pushing them farther and farther away from the actual event that generated them. If I had done so, it seemed to me that, in this case, the people I was writing about would have no agency and would become vulnerable.

Also, I discovered I could not *imagine* a situation that I was, in fact, so closely involved in and this discovery did influence my poetics and I made a conscious decision to use only what was true, and this fact, perhaps strangely, made me simplify many of the poems. I say strangely because, if you redraft a poem to make it simpler, you risk losing the material that relates it to the real experience it describes. I found that process arduous, choosing what facts to include. The other difficulty was that, while I can write simply, I often prefer to add complications to my poetics, hide words within words, enjamb to enhance possible meanings, for example. Here though, I could not let myself indulge in linguistic novelty for its own sake. I had only to clarify my experience, my feelings, my thoughts and those of my partner. I don't normally care too much for clarity. I like blur in a poem; it's like the taste in a meal. I felt *A Pair of Three* could become a plain lettuce and tomato salad, no dressing, no blurring the taste. Simplicity makes powerful poetry in the hands of, say, a poet laureate who must represent and communicate with the nation as a whole – Ada Limon, the current US laureate, for example. Her work is simple yet extraordinarily powerful. Needless to say, I didn't always achieve such simplicity; at a certain stage of creation, at the point when I take a poem seriously, blur is what my mind struggles with; from then on it infests every line I write.

So I struggled towards clarity. For example, 'The Welcome' was originally, before *A Pair of Three* had been developed, a long description of a caller; it was not a fascinating poem, and I had no idea (common to my usual practice) why I wanted to write it, to write about someone knocking on the front door. I tried to jazz it up with references to doorstep selling, neighbours calling unexpectedly. It was tedious, even as I played with technique. Once the set was forming, I realised the doorstep image was borne from the same pair of dreams as 'The Visitor'. 'The Visitor' originated in a dream I had had years before, that was so vivid and meaningful to me I have never forgotten it. I was sitting at home, kettle on, very happy, working at a table, when I heard a knock. I looked out of the window and saw Jude, laden with shopping bags, wanting some help from Keith. He wasn't there. She unlocked the door and came in; I then realised with a massive shock that it was her home I sat in, not mine. I thought I must escape from this house; she must not think I have taken it over. I slid past her on the stair. I was horrified and still revisit the dream as you might do the memory of a short agonising horror film.

'The Welcome' presents a similar horror story; I heard the knock, looked out of the window, saw a woman in Jude's floaty scarf and tough boots (clothes in our wardrobe that Keith took a while to let go). I thought desperately, in the dream, of not opening the door. But I decided I had to open it and so woke up in distress, cutting short the dream as I raised the latch. It was a short, bare dream. Later, during the process that transmuted a few muddled stanzas about an unknown caller to the house, I found that simplifying the poetic form kept the actuality, the intense feeling, of the dream. I used syllabics, intending it as a numbering device to underline meaning: the poem is four stanzas, each one a tercet, to indicate that, though in this poem there are two protagonists, the situation is made complex by a third person. The tercets have a syllabic pattern, 6/4/4. The first line of six syllables represents, as a multiple, the pair of three. The second and third lines of four syllables represent, as multiples of two, the two protagonists. Both groups are doubled, simply to give my words room, but also to hint at the widespread nature of this situation.

CE: Tell me about the syllabics in these poems. On a second read through the first half, it seems there's a patterning....

CC: I use syllabics when the poem seems to benefit from patterning that is not so rhythmic as iambic pentameter, for example, but does need tight linear and/or stanzaic control.

My use of syllabics is usually as a stanza pattern, and each poem works out its own pattern as I revise, much as Marianne Moore worked out stanza patterns in her early work. There might, of course, be only one stanza as in 'I Think Heaven Must Co-opt Hell for Help' (p.49). This poem begins with a grand image that is enclosed in a tight space: 'Evening. A cathedral tucked down a close...' I made the repeating syllabic pattern of one long line of eleven syllables and one short line of five. The imagery continues to reflect largeness that is contained as in the fourth and fifth lines: 'At the iron gate / gargoyles guard a saint who throws wide her warm arms' (p. 49).

The sound of syllabically controlled lines can be awkward, and I usually make poems syllabic that deal with awkwardness of some kind. For example, 'Those Keys' (p.35), depicts a situation where the narrator is locked in the garden and out of the house by a forgetful partner. The line-count pattern that eventually worked is one of four-line stanzas of 4/9/6/4 syllables, again multiples of two and three syllables in each stanza. The two protagonists, myself and my partner, are fixed apart, as are lines 1 and 4 in the first stanza. Inside this experience of enforced separation, the pairs of three begin to consider their emotional reality and, as they do so, the position of the syllabic line count changes. Stanza four is 4/4/6/9 (p.35):

> That bad thing I
> would not face – I
> have to think about it.
> I'll kneel to think. I'll pluck back thick stalks.

The first two lines bunch up awkwardly, each being four syllables. The narrator has to face her desire to turn away from the feeling of being abandoned; each of the two lines ends in 'I'. Calmness descends in line three as the narrator accepts what she must do – face the bad thing, and those two 'I's reappear in the last line where they have been accepted and absorbed into the reality of the emotional situation. Also, that last line breathes out, relaxes, even though the single-syllable words demonstrate that she must take one step at a time to come to terms with being locked out. Here is the last stanza (p.35):

> Two mice eyes glint.
> Fox rat death lurk.
> He clutches the cold keys while he hums:
> 'Where has she gone?'

There are three lines with four syllables, suggesting the pair (multiples of two syllables) of three (lines). For now, the lost wife has gone despite the worlds of other beings – fox rat mice – lurking. But the nine-syllable line tucked inside the stanza suggests that my partner is still searching for his lost love, and it is he who asks the final question that so terrifies his new partner: 'Where has she gone?'

CE: Is it because of the more freighted personal subject matter that nonsense seems to play less of a role in this book?

CC: Certainly, there is a question of tone in any collection. Much of this collection is sad; elegy and lament, styles that are interwoven with love, are the most typical here. Nonsense does not thrive in this context, and I left some nonsense poems out.

I didn't want to lighten the sense of loss in these poems: someone much loved has died. If I put too much humour in, there would be an embarrassment for the reader as well as for my family. While I claim to consider nothing but the poem while I am writing, I do believe in not doing damage – especially not to people I love. If I truly want to consider nothing but the poem, I will not write about pain that affects people directly, people I am close to who have no power to control my publications. I asked particularly for my stepdaughters' and partner's thoughts on the book and would have taken those into consideration if they had felt uncomfortable with my exposing their mother/wife in this way.

There are only two poems in this collection that express loss humorously: 'Lost in Thought' and 'The Us'. They are placed together in the centre of the book; I think of beginnings and endings of books as the more important parts. As well as situating them almost out of sight, their placement suggests their central importance. 'The Us', a title phrase that encompasses the book's theme, concludes with a physicist's analysis of the evolution of love: 'Order in the universe increased tremendously / till love became an evolutionary principle.' (p.42). The situation of the poem conveys the humour, with a narrator running downstairs to question her partner about 'the us'.

I agonised more over whether to include 'Lost in Thought', and perhaps that is because it is a prose poem in which the narrator is trying to find a child who is hiding while also working as an intellectual nonsense poem. This approach, ratiocinative and/or analytic, is nonsensically constructed: 'Is seriousness a growing problem for outdoor bowls?' (p.39). I decided such an odd approach to the book's theme was a valuable decompression, a place to relax the essential tragedy of a dead partner. Throughout the poem the lost partner, seen as a child, is not visible, but the narrator searches in every stanza: 'Where are you?' she calls 'Where are you?' While she searches, as a mother searches for a child, she can't calm the nonsense-analysis in her mind: 'There is spending being spent and having been spent. *Hold it right now.* And then again Søren Kierkegaard explained thrillingly – explanations engender doubt.' It is clear, I think, that the poem is a trip into Hades: 'The dead are not doing what they are told. There is looking for them calling and messaging. Sometimes she hides, tiny as the ghost spider *Anyphaenidae.*' The mind, says this poem, provides its own version of hell for the bereaved.

CE: Would you talk me through the elliptical poem, 'I Saw a Crowd of Weird Birds' (p.56)?

CC: This, like all of these poems, is derived from an experience of a close relative of mine; she has spoken of this event many times, and it is of great importance to her. She was thinking of her lost partner, and, as she felt the loss, she looked out of the window and saw a large group of birds drop onto her lawn. She had never seen a great crowd land on the lawn like that and turned away to pick up a camera. When she turned back, they had disappeared. She felt it was a visitation of souls, particularly her partner's soul, and that it was comforting. To me, the incident seems full of longing, to the point that the natural world, other beings, are drawn to it. Her longing filled the garden, and birds were pulled out of the sky by the intensity of her feeling.

I decided to show the coupling that goes on after a partner is lost. Each line in the first four lines has the same word or near-derivative repeated at the end: 'ground. Ground'; 'away. Away'; 'None. No one'; 'not. Not'. This coupled vision is a denial of the single soul; those who have partners are paired for eternity. Those lines are descriptive of the crowd of birds, and the narrator then uses the imperative for the second and third stanza:

> Find out confined out
> in as much *always* as there is there
> if there is no there there
> or no no end.

Now that the narrator has begun to question the existence of the lost partner, the repetitive line ending spreads across the whole line. The final line is a call to the lost partner both to come back and report on what is 'there' after death, as a soul, but also to rise from the dead, Lazarus-like: 'Then make your comeback, Come back here.' Seeing birds, butterflies, or moths that have crossed your path, as representing the one you have lost is a feature of mourning, in my experience.

CE: In some respects, this collection could be called 'love poetry'. Would you agree with that classification? Did you have any love poems in mind as you were working on this collection?

CC: I think of this book as love poetry: that is, poetry borne of love, of the effort to love. It is hard to explain the complexity of any love relationship without sounding as though I believe lovers should be passive and accept damage from the relationship. I don't think that at all. I am referring to poetry that encounters the dark night of the soul, absence and even torment, as characteristics of love at a certain level of commitment to a relationship. A new lover, as the relationship goes on, finds that the deepest reality of their partner holds experiences that are separate from them and, in that separation, painful. The lover must ask themself, 'is this wrong for me because this is hurting me?' and even contemplate leaving the relationship. The relationship could grow stronger, though, when both lovers have exposed their deeper agonies, each to each. I am thinking of poems such as 'Love' (George Herbert), 'The Voice' (Thomas

Hardy), 'Valentine' (Carol Ann Duffy), 'Two in the Campagna' (Robert Browning), and countless others. It was almost a relief to write about that central lyrical subject, lost love, as the central theme of a collection. So, as I've said, this collection marked a development for me, and, hauntingly, the same sense of abandonment has appeared in *Real Lear*, the collection that follows *A Pair of Three*.

REFERENCES

Crowther, C. (2022) *A Pair of Three*. Bristol: Shearsman Books.

Real Lear: New and Selected Poems
(Shearsman, 2024)

CE: Tell me about the new poems in *Real Lear*. Who are Lady Lear and the Corybant girls?

CC: Lady Lear is my version of the old king, Lear, not a blow by blow account of the Shakespeare story, but a picture of the age when Lear is separated from her family, wandering in the dark and cold. The poems play with the meanings of love and duty and abandonment. 'Those Corybant girls' (in 'Lady Lear Dreams, Half-wakes and Can't Remember') refers to the followers of the mother-goddess Cybele; the details, the kitchen, the back road, the snowy village green, sketch the life of a young mother, and the poem ends with a meditation on the worth of youth. All the new poems look at the materiality of morality in the context of (imminent) death. Lear is best known as a man: I wanted to explore how a woman would suffer in old age, in the gradual abandonment of life, which is what age is.

CE: From the start, the poems appear more sound-led with playful repetitions of sound. Are they all syllabic?

CC: Not all of them, but syllabics is the dominant form in the set. Some syllabically constructed poems have lines that differ from the overall pattern ('Hazards and Thrown Humans', for example) though not by many syllables. I don't believe a syllabic poem has to be exact on every line. There are many reasons why you might want to vary the number of syllables on a line: the meaning of that line within the poem's narrative is disruption, or extension, for example, as in 'Hazards'. Readers can detect a pattern, learn to expect it, and then enjoy a subtle difference here and there. Sound is vital in poetry even in page poetry like mine. Words have meanings but also sounds that may accord with their meaning or strangely differ. 'Like', for example, a positive word, sounds cutting. 'Pain' sounds gentle, soothing even. Organising the sounds of a poem challenges me hugely. I hear the title, *Real Lear*, like the recoil that the letters make: it's almost a palindrome. The recoil is gentle, a rocking motion I could repeat over and over like a lullaby. That gives me a calm sensation, reassurance.

Real Lear suggests that the Lear we know from myth and history is unreal. Anyway, in my poems, Lear is a woman and more real to me for that.

CE: How do you find a syllabic form? To be more precise, how did you come to the form of 'Falling from the Surface of the World *or* Lear's Rescue'?

CC: My process discovers the form. I do the same process with every poem I write. First, I pour out a pile of words, the meanings accrue as the heap grows, the sounds drive the words, and I end up with a few pages of phrases, single words, sentences. I mess around with these pages for days, add some words, take some away. Then I put it in the metaphorical drawer for some weeks. When I take it out and reread, after an absence, I hear clearly the phrases/sentences I like, the ones that are going to dominate the poem. I lay those out on separate lines. I count how many syllables are in each line, and I have set my first syllabic pattern for the poem. This can be changed through the redrafting process, for all sorts of reasons: to illustrate the poem's narrative, maybe, a diminishing set of syllabic lines would work. Sometimes the poem might abandon its syllabic pattern.

CE: Tell me about when you began writing fatrasies and what attracted you to the form.

CC: I was starting to write a set of poems dealing with the body, particularly the layer of fat that keeps us warm and has been so much maligned in Western culture. I had worked for some years in the weight management industry and knew a bit about the science of adipose tissue as well as about the fear of fat and the emotions, negative and positive, connected with it. While I was drafting and redrafting, I found, serendipitously, that there was a thirteenth-century poetic form called a *fatrasie*. It has an initial couplet followed by an eleven-line section, a syllabic pattern and an end-rhyme pattern. It began as a comic entertainment for the French aristocracy, became hugely popular and then settled down in the fourteenth century with a much more pious tone (though nonsense fatrasies continued to be written). It seems to have disappeared about a hundred years later. I liked the unevenness and relative shortness of eleven lines and started to pull my body fat poems into that number of lines. But what fascinated and challenged me most was another device the fatras uses: the introductory couplet is composed of the first and last line of the following eleven lines. Thus, including the couplet, a fatras is typically a thirteen-line poem.

This couplet is fascinating to write. There is one meaning in the first line of a poem, another meaning in the last line, and a third meaning built into those two lines when they are placed next to each other. The couplet can enjamb, making even more meanings. Or the poet can alter a word or two in either line, or change the punctuation to alter meaning. Within a short form, the possibilities are many. Of course, once you are working with this form, as with any form, you are encouraged by its requirements to enlarge the poem's territory, to push it onwards, and I very often finish with a fatras that is 'about' something very different from the first draft.

I like the fatras form so much that now I use it as a stage in the development of every poem. By the way, I don't even attempt the rhyme pattern that those clever mediaeval poets used. Maybe one day…

CE: 'Lear's Inwit' is a surreal prose poem, the Report come to consciousness. Does 'inwit' imply this report is Lear's conscience?

CC: Yes, absolutely. You can read this poem in different ways, I hope, but I was trying to engage with the opportunity for an assessment, a critiquing, of a past life, that age offers. The last self I have will make an account of itself, will look at how it has been made, will try to say what its message is, though, as the ending of the poem shows, I think, it is not for any one of us to know exactly what others will learn from us. If anything. The Report is humbled and still must try to speak. I wrote it during lockdown, from 2020 to 2022. What a surreal time that was. I was in a more meditative state than I'd ever been, for longer hours in the day, and these Lear poems belong to that period of fear and judgement from outside and inside. It is also an after-death story; there are many sorts of judgments. I was brought up a Catholic and was taught that purgatory, that self-reflective after-death period, is an interesting state!

CE: I'm intrigued by the choice of 'Soundsunder' as your final poem. Would you comment on that choice?

CC: I have written many poems about shyness. Maybe there's a future collection there? It's a hard state to describe, and shyness does not mean that you retreat from people necessarily, only that you are self-conscious and stressed while in their presence. I placed the poem at the end because I wanted to acknowledge the reader, that important person who gives me time to speak, who waits for me to gather myself, who lets me say where I am in this surreal world. If there's an 'us' in a poetry collection, it has to be formed of poet and reader.

But there is another aspect of this poem. Some years ago, I started to attend Quaker meetings. I have never joined, not being a joiner, but there are many things about Quaker practice that I like. Silence is one, a huge attraction. You simply sit with other people in a circle and stay, largely, silent. Occasionally, someone is driven to speak briefly to the group, another interesting part of Quaker practice. I have never, in all the eleven years I've attended Quaker meetings, ever spoken in the meeting. Some of the description of the group, the silence, and the 'hush of us' comes from this experience. Also, as Lear, I must come in out of the cold, and this poem says that: 'it's time to talk / to others / besides yourself'. I am talking to myself there, but also it's an exhortation to those who, like me, withhold themselves, for whatever reason. It's noticeable how, in old age, people value and try to be with old friends as much as possible. There is no judgement among old friends, I have found. Actually, there is no need to talk, either. There is an 'our of self', and we older people know about that.

CE: A *Selected Poems* feels like a poetic career's culmination, and yet one hopes there is more to come. What are you working on now?

CC: I can't imagine not writing poems. The interesting thing about publishing a collection is that, by the time it comes out, the poet is often well underway with the next book. For my next collection, I have conceptualised and am developing several poems that explore the spiritual side of current social mores and events. To vivify the poems, I've invented a character with a recognisable religious title but who doesn't necessarily belong to any particular sect. As I was brought up in a devoutly Catholic home, I have many experiences and impressions that will flesh out this character, though she isn't herself a Catholic. When the poems have settled a bit – in perhaps a year's time – I will do some deeper research into thinkers who have interested me for years: Etty Hillesum, Simone Weil, Margaret Fox. Perhaps I'll have a retreat or, most enjoyably, find a residency in an appropriate religious setting. Then I'll recast and rewrite the poems and, no doubt, write some more.

I wonder if this is one of the needs of older age, to sort out where you are, soulside. I am influenced in this respect by Gillian Allnutt's profound poetry, among many others. The problem is that, inevitably, writing about such material, you must encounter, somehow account for, describe, even lyricise, evil. So, while I treat writing poems as a marvellous game, I expect this next book to be punishing to write. Maybe I'll want to give up then?

REFERENCES

Crowther, C. (2024) *Real Lear: New & Selected Poems*. Bristol: Shearsman Books.

Acknowledgements

A number of these essays originally appeared in different forms as talks or articles. 'The Resurrected Line: Periodicity and the Grandmother Poem' began as a talk given at the British and Irish Contemporary Poetry Conference at St Anne's College, Oxford, in September 2006, and appeared in *British and Irish Contemporary Poetry*. 'A Poet's Sense of Nonsense' originated in a series of lectures given at *Poetry and Voice: A Creative and Critical Conference* at the University of Chichester, June 2010, and adapted for a lecture at the Oxford Creative Writing Diploma Summer School, August 2023. 'Confessing to Syllabics' was published originally as 'Psychosyllabics' in *PN Review* 229 (2016) and republished online in *Poetry Daily*. It was later adapted for a lecture given at Oxford Creative Writing Diploma Summer School, August 2022. 'Veronica Forrest-Thomson, Modernism and Me' was originally given as a talk at the StAnza International Poetry Festival, 10 March 2022. Grateful thanks to the conference organisers and journal editors who have listened to, read and discussed these essays with me.

Reviews in this collection first appeared in *London Magazine*, *Long Poem Magazine*, *Magma*, *Poetry London*, *Poetry Review*, and *Poetry Wales*.

This collection of essays would not have begun life without the support of Shearsman Books' publisher, Tony Frazer. For his long-term confidence in my work, I am deeply grateful. Heartfelt thanks also go to my ever-calm partner Keith Barnham, and to Anne Berkeley, Linda Black, Lorna Dowell, Rhona McAdam, Sue Rose, and Tamar Yoseloff for their constant encouragement in deviating from poetry and tackling prose. Lastly, for her extraordinary professionalism, assiduity, intelligence and good humour during the tough times, huge thanks to Carrie Etter.

Index

www.ingramcontent.com/pod-product-compliance
Lightning Source LLC
Chambersburg PA
CBHW030035030726
47500CB00001B/118